A CHILD INTO THE WORLD

A Guide to Making Your Kids Confident, Independent, and Self-Reliant Through Traveling

Dr. Robert J. Walker, Jr.

A CHILD INTO THE WORLD © 2024

All rights reserved. No part of this book may be reproduced in any form or by any electronic or mechanical means, including information storage and retrieval systems, without permission in writing from the author. This book was professionally written, edited, and formatted. It is not a pre-published work and remains the copyrighted property of the author.

The information provided in this book is designed to provide helpful information on the subjects discussed. The author's books are only meant to give the reader the basic knowledge of specific topics without any guarantees concerning results. This book is for educational and entertainment purposes only. While most care has been taken in compiling the information contained in this book, no responsibility can be accepted by the author for any errors or omissions that may be made. Neither can any liability be accepted by the publisher for any damages, losses, or costs resulting from using the information contained within these pages.

All trademarks and registered trademarks appearing in this book are the property of their respective owners and are used only to describe the products provided directly. Every effort has been made to appropriately capitalize, punctuate, identify, and attribute trademarks and register where appropriate according to industry standards.

Printed in the United States of America

ISBN: 979-8-3485-5066-0

10 9 8 7 6 5 4 3 2 1

EMPIRE PUBLISHING
www.empirebookpublishing.com

Dedication

This book is lovingly dedicated to two extraordinary souls who have left an indelible mark on my heart and this world—my cherished daughter, Ryeshia Walker, and my beloved mother, Barbara Wallace Robinson.

Ryeshia embraced life's journeys with boundless curiosity and courage until her untimely departure at the tender age of 24. With her radiant smile and contagious laugh, she brought light to every room. As a child, her sense of adventure knew no bounds, and she would talk for hours about the places she dreamed of exploring one day. She taught me that every moment is a gift and to live each day to the fullest.

My mother, Barbara, was the steadfast pillar of our family. Throughout my childhood and beyond, her guidance, empathy, and spiritual strength sustained us through every challenge. As a teacher, she ignited curiosity in  her students and brought history to life in the classroom. Outside of work, she could often be found in the garden, where she cultivated not only flowers but also compassion and wisdom in all who knew her. Her unconditional love and enduring lessons are gifts that will shape me for life. Other than teaching, she enjoyed spending time with her grand children and decorating her house.

This book is my tribute to you both. Through these pages, may your legacy continue to guide and inspire parents to venture beyond their doorsteps with their children, discovering not just new places but new depths to the bonds they share. Your memories are the wings upon which this message flies, reaching hearts and kindling flames of adventure in honor of the love and lessons you've left behind.

Acknowledgment

I am overwhelmed with gratitude for the countless individuals who have played a pivotal role in shaping both my life and the journey of this book. To each of you, I extend my heartfelt appreciation and profound acknowledgments.

First and foremost, I offer my deepest gratitude to the **Divine**, whose unwavering presence, guidance, and grace have been the cornerstone of my existence. Your love and wisdom have illuminated my path, guiding me through both challenges and triumphs.

To my beloved parents, **Barbara Wallace Robinson** and **Robert Walker Sr.**, whose enduring love, wisdom, and unwavering belief in me continue to shape my journey, even in their physical absence, I am forever grateful. Your legacy of resilience and determination lives on in my heart, inspiring me to reach for the stars.

To my cherished siblings, **Eric**, **Kris**, **Keryl**, and **Jessica**, your unconditional love, camaraderie, and shared laughter have been the threads that bind our hearts together. Your presence in my life has brought me immense joy and strength.

To my precious daughters, **Ryeshia** (deceased), **Sydney**, and **Olivia**, your love, light, and indomitable spirits have enriched my life beyond measure. Though Ryeshia may no longer be with us in body, her presence remains eternally felt, a beacon of love and inspiration guiding our family forward.

*To my beloved wife, **Irina**, your love, support, and unwavering belief in me have been my greatest blessings. Your presence in my life is a constant reminder of the beauty of love and companionship.*

*To my **family and friends**, whose love, encouragement, and unwavering support have sustained me through every trial and triumph, I am eternally grateful. Your belief in me has been a source of strength and inspiration.*

*To my fraternity brothers of **Kappa Alpha Psi Fraternity, Inc.**, your brotherhood, camaraderie, and unwavering support have been a source of strength and inspiration. Together, we have uplifted each other, celebrated achievements, and stood firm in times of adversity, and for that, I am forever grateful.*

To all those who have offered their support, encouragement, and wisdom along the way, I extend my heartfelt gratitude. Your belief in me and this project has been a guiding light, propelling me forward even in the face of adversity.

Finally, to the readers who embark on this journey with me, I extend my most profound appreciation for your interest and support. May the words within these pages resonate with you, inspire you, and remind you of the boundless potential within every child.

About the Author

Robert Walker Jr. is a renowned mediator, consultant, and retired UPS executive. With over 30 years of experience managing large-scale operations, Robert brings a wealth of leadership knowledge to resolving conflicts and driving organizational transformation.

Robert began his career in 1985 working at UPS, where he steadily took on increasing responsibility roles. Over the years at UPS, Robert proved himself as a dynamic leader, receiving numerous accolades and recognition awards for his outstanding performance leading various high-profile territories. As a Congressional Awareness Coordinator, Robert also played a pivotal role in securing important legislation.

In 2019, after dedicating over three decades to UPS, Robert retired from the company. That same year, he founded Walker Mediation & Consulting with the goal of helping businesses, executives, and individuals overcome disputes through peaceful mediation. Robert received his Doctorate in Business Administration from National University.

Beyond dispute resolution, Robert also works closely with clients to develop strategies that maximize efficiency, mitigate risk, and optimize workplace culture. With expertise spanning finance, logistics, human resources, and more, Robert guides organizational transformations that elevate performance.

A dedicated community advocate, Robert has served on boards for esteemed groups like the Urban League and the American Red Cross. He is also actively involved with Kappa Alpha Psi Fraternity as a mentor. Robert obtained his bachelor's degree from Albany State University and MBA from Nova Southeastern University, and he is a certified mediator by the Florida Supreme Court.

When not leading his practice, He enjoys traveling and spending time with his family. Robert enjoys spending quality time with his wife, Irina, and his daughters, Sydney and Olivia. In this book, Robert lends his invaluable insight on conflict resolution and leveraging mediation to impact business and interpersonal relationships positively.

Contents

Dedication iii
Acknowledgment v
About the Author vii
Introduction xi
Chapter 1 Opening Minds to New Horizons 1
    Fostering Growth in Young Age 4
    The Adventure of Becoming You 7
Chapter 2 Crafting the Ideal Itinerary for Little Feet 10
    Choosing Child-Centric Destinations 11
    Why Some Places Mesmerize Young Minds More Than Others 12
    Integrating Educational Opportunities with Entertainment 13
    The Balance Between Adventure and Safety in Selecting Locations 14
    Interactive Itineraries 16
    Designing a Kid-Approved Agenda That Involves Their Input .. 17
    Structuring Days with Flexibility, Incorporating Both High-Energy Activities and Rest 18
    Making Room for Spontaneous Exploration Alongside Planned Visits 19
    Safety Through Preparation 20
    Tools and Practices for Security in Unfamiliar Environments .. 21
    Preparing for Common Travel Mishaps with a Child-Centered Approach 23
Chapter 3 Education on the Go 25
    Real-World Learning Unleashed 27
    Experiential Learning 28
    Enhancing Problem-Solving and Adaptability 29
    The Tapestry of Cultures 31

Curating Authentic Experiences... 32
Practical Language Adventures... 33
Making History Accessible 35
Chapter 4 Budget Travelling with Children................................... 38
Smart Savings Secrets.. 40
Rewards Programs and Memberships 41
Living Like a Local 42
Hidden Gem Destinations 43
Innovative Entertainment on a Budget..................................... 45
Chapter 5 Packing Tips and Tricks 48
Interactive Packing Checklists 50
The Travel Journal Kit.. 52
The Essential Emergency Kit 54
Chapter 6 Navigating Travel Challenges 57
Transforming Jet Lag into a Journey Adjustment Tool 59
A Creative Approach to Managing Meltdowns 60
Understand the 'Why' Behind Meltdowns................................61
Strategies That Work 62
Overcoming the Challenge of Lost Stuff 64
The Art of Preparation.. 64
Turning Losses into Learning Opportunities 65
The Backup Plan 65
Navigating Missed Schedules... 67
The Adventure of Staying Healthy 69
Chapter 7 Engaging Activities for Children 72
Nurturing Naturalists - The Great Outdoors as a Classroom 73
Decoding History and Culture Through Museums 75
The Art of Travel Journaling 78
Hands-on Experiences with Local Crafts and Cuisine 81

Chapter 8 The Art of Slow Travel 84

    The Philosophy of Slow Travel 85

    Patience as a Travel Companion 89

Chapter 9 Harnessing Technology for Enhanced Travel Experiences 92

    The Art of Digital Storytelling 96

    Smart Travel - Technology as Your Ultimate Trip Companion 99

Chapter 10 Weaving Memories Into Stories - The Journey Beyond 102

    Global Citizenship Through Reflection 104

    Our Children Will Thank Us 106

    The Path Forward 109

Chapter 11 Guide Right - Preparing a Child for Life 113

    Financial Responsibility 114

    Bank Accounts 115

    Investing 117

    Understanding Taxes 119

    Golden Nuggets 120

Chapter 12 Connection with God for Life 124

    The Role of the Church 125

    Pray Before You Go to Bed 128

    Say Grace Before You Eat 130

    Thank God for His Blessing 132

Chapter 13 Participation in Sports or Other Activities 135

    Get Involved at an Early Age 136

    Empowering Choices - Letting Your Child Lead 138

    Show Your Support 141

Chapter 14 There Will Be Mistakes 143

Epilogue 147

References..148

Introduction

In the heart of every child lies an insatiable curiosity about the world around them. This curiosity, if nurtured through travel, can transform their view of the world and themselves.

Travel, often perceived as a luxury, is, in fact, an investment in the future. When Sydney and Olivia, my two daughters, set their feet on lands far from home, they didn't just collect souvenirs; they gathered perspectives.

Sydney's eyes sparkled with the same wonder beneath the Eiffel Tower as they did when exploring the cultural depths of Helsinki, while Olivia's young mind absorbed the diverse heritage of Russia during her visit. Their journeys were not just about the places they visited; they were about the widening of their worldviews and the deepening of their empathy.

The saddest regret of my life is not having shared the gift of travel with my oldest daughter before she passed away. This regret fuels my resolve to advocate for travel as an essential ingredient in a child's development.

Travel changes focus. Kids with wanderlust look beyond the streets of their neighborhood; they envision a world of possibilities. It introduces them to role models who wield pens and brushes rather than guns and deals. It teaches them that their dreams need not be confined by their ZIP codes.

This book lays out a blueprint for parents, primarily single and low-income parents, to make travel accessible. It debunks myths about the cost of travel, offering practical advice on how to explore the world on a shoestring budget. Real-life examples, including the strategies my wife and I employed to expose Sydney and Olivia to global cultures, will inspire others to take action.

Moreover, this book emphasizes the positive impact of travel on a child's development. From improved cognitive abilities to enhanced social skills and increased empathy, the benefits of travel are limitless. It also addresses challenges that may arise during travels, such as culture shock and homesickness, and provides tips on how to overcome them.

This book reveals how exposure to new cultures, environments, and experiences can pivot the life trajectory of at-risk children toward boundless potential.

Travel is more affordable now than it has ever been. The digital age offers myriad resources to slash travel costs, from flight comparison sites to home-sharing platforms. The key lies in prioritizing experiences over material possessions. A weekend getaway to a nearby city, rich in history and culture, can be as impactful as a trip across the ocean. It's about showing children the diversity of the world and teaching them that, despite our differences, we share common dreams and challenges.

Remembering my first flight at the age of 8 and the ripples it created in my young mind, it's clear that the skies we soar through can lift us above the constraints of our immediate environments.

However, the stark reality remains that many never taste this freedom. Encounters with prejudice, like the one my family faced when considering a vacation home, further paint the complex canvas of travel for minorities. But it is in the conquering of these challenges that the true power of travel is revealed.

I also want to touch on a point very close to my heart—the experience of being the only person of color on international flights underscores a concerning trend: the scarcity of minorities in traveler demographics. This is not just a reflection of economic hurdles but also of a deeply embedded notion that travel is out of reach for many.

While writing this, I'm reminded of a quote from Michelle Obama, "Don't ever underestimate the importance you can have *because history has shown us that courage can be contagious and hope can take on a life of its own.*"

My childhood, albeit filled with more travel opportunities than many of my friends, was marked by budget-conscious decisions. From camping in Fort Gaines, GA, to witnessing baseball in Atlanta, the essence wasn't in the grandeur of the destinations but in the richness of experiences. That is precisely what I want to instill in parents—that travel is an opportunity for growth and learning, regardless of one's financial circumstances.

Before we go further, I want to tell you a bit about myself. I genuinely have a passion for travel and seeing new things. To date, I've visited 63 countries, a statistic that stands in stark contrast to many kids I grew up with who never traveled outside our local area.

Travel was indeed costly when I was growing up. Coming from a middle-class family with both parents as teachers and being the oldest of three brothers, I experienced firsthand the financial juggling required to explore the world. I am 1 year older than one brother and 12 years older than my youngest brother, who was only 2 when our parents divorced.

Our family travels were modest but meaningful. Trips with my parents often involved camping and fishing in Fort Gaines, GA—a 2-hour drive from our home. Other memorable journeys included a 5-hour drive to Disney in Orlando, FL, an 8-hour drive to visit family in Miami (I still remember taking a coconut back to my elementary school for show and tell, much to the excitement of my classmates), and a 4-hour drive to Panama City Beach. There was even an attempt to buy a vacation home in Destin, FL, near Panama City, which ended abruptly when my father was rudely turned away by a homeowner who suggested we look in Detroit instead.

Another pivotal moment in my travel experiences, which further supports the thesis that early exposure to travel can significantly impact a child's likelihood of attaining post-secondary education and succeeding in life, occurred during a family trip to Colorado Springs. Along with my mother, stepfather, my two brothers, Eric and Kris, and my mother's two sisters and their families, we embarked on an arduous

1,568-mile drive from Albany, GA. Our destination was to visit my mom's oldest brother and his family. One of the highlights of this trip was visiting Pikes Peak, a moment that remains etched in my memory for its breathtaking views and the sense of adventure it instilled in us.

This experience, much like the others detailed in this book, emphasizes how travel, regardless of its scale or the extravagance of the destination, enriches a child's life. Venturing far from the familiar surroundings of home to the majestic peaks of Colorado Springs not only broadened our geographical horizons but also exposed us to new cultures, histories, and perspectives.

Amidst these personal anecdotes of travel and the lessons they've imparted, it's essential to acknowledge the diverse paths that have shaped my perspective on life and success. One such experience began in my high school years, further underlining the importance of seizing opportunities and the role of mentors in guiding us.

I worked as a meat cutter from the age of 16, a job I secured thanks to my high VOCA teacher, Mr. Charles Price. This position wasn't just a job; it presented a potential career path, especially as I progressed to become the meat department manager at one of the largest grocery stores in town while in college. The financial independence it offered was significant—I was making as much as my mother, who held a master's degree and was a seasoned teacher. Despite the lucrative aspect, my mother encouraged me to pursue my education further and keep my options open.

During this period, my engagement with the local semi-pro baseball team and discussions with my best friend, Rod Griffin, brought a new opportunity my way. Rod suggested exploring a role with UPS that aligned with my college schedule and would allow me to continue my education while working. This part-time job at UPS unfolded an entirely new chapter in my life.

It wasn't just about the job; it was about the people I met who had traveled the world and shared their stories, expanding my understanding of what was possible. My division manager, Bill Thompson, became a mentor who not only taught me about the intricacies of finance but also how to leverage company stock to my benefit. This phase marked a significant transition in my life, illustrating how varied experiences and the people we encounter can profoundly impact our worldview, much like the travels I cherished so deeply.

Despite the financial struggles and the lengthy, cramped car rides, the wealth of experiences and learning this trip offered was invaluable. It is experiences like these, I believe, that plant the seeds of curiosity, ambition, and a desire for learning in young minds, driving them toward higher education and success in life, transcending the confines of their immediate environment.

Despite these experiences, or perhaps because of them, travel has been a profound teacher. My parents ensured we attended an Atlanta Braves baseball game every year, with just a 3-hour drive. The first time I flew was around eight years old, on a trip to New York with my mother to visit her aunt. My first trip out of the country came in 1987 to the Bahamas, shortly after completing my undergraduate degree—a milestone that marked the beginning of my global adventures.

This is not merely a book; it's a movement. It's a call to arms for parents, guardians, and educators to break the chains of routine and dare to explore the world. Within these pages, you'll find not just anecdotes but actionable steps to make travel a reality for the children in your life.

In essence, travel is like a book with infinite pages. Each trip turns a new page, revealing lessons, adventures, and mysteries. Just as no two destinations are the same, no two journeys within these pages will be identical.

Yet, the outcome remains consistent—travel molds children into global citizens armed with compassion, understanding, and an unquenchable thirst for knowledge. In every corner of the world, there are stories waiting to be discovered, adventures waiting to be lived, and lessons waiting to be learned. It's time to turn the page.

Chapter 1
Opening Minds to New Horizons

Imagine, if you will, a world where passports are as prized as the latest video game console, where tales of adventure replace bedtime stories, and where young explorers are the heroes of their own narratives. This isn't just a fanciful musing; it's the heart and soul of what travel can do for a child's development.

Travel isn't merely about hopping from one landmark to another or ticking off destinations on a list. It's about the sparkle in a child's eye when they try gelato for the first time on a cobblestone street in Italy or the hands-on history lesson they get wandering through the ruins of Machu Picchu. It's about their mind expanding faster than their passport fills up with stamps as they encounter new languages, foods, and ways of life.

Take Lucy, for instance, a 10-year-old from a small town whose first trip abroad was to Japan. Overwhelmed? Slightly. Fascinated? Absolutely. She learned to say "thank you" in Japanese, spent hours watching the meticulous preparation of sushi, and came back with stories that rivaled her entire year's worth of school experiences. Then there's Jamal, who, after a family trip to Kenya, started a fundraiser at his school to help protect endangered animals he'd seen on a safari.

During the early formative years, travel can play a pivotal role in shaping young minds. Psychologists call it "experiential learning," which is a fancy way of saying that when we encounter something new, we learn better (1). It's not just about sitting in classrooms and listening to lectures; it's about being fully immersed in experiences that foster growth and development.

Let's bring it full circle—remember that glittering tapestry of interconnected stories we talked about earlier? Travel helps children see that tapestry, connect the threads of their own stories, and understand that they are a vital part of this beautiful world. It's not just about opening minds to new horizons; it's about helping them discover themselves and their place in the world.

These aren't just vacations; they're life lessons in curiosity and the interconnectedness of our world. When children like Lucy and Jamal travel, they're not just tourists—they're tiny ambassadors learning the fine art of cultural appreciation and global stewardship.

Through travel, children learn that the world is more significant than their backyard and far more varied than what they see on TV. It's in the bustling markets, the quiet museums, the ancient forests, and the vibrant city streets that they find lessons that stick—the kind of education that no textbook can provide.

I've decided to open the chapter with a note of curiosity because that is what children are born with and what travel feeds. As a young reader, I'm sure you're bubbling with questions like "What kind of adventures can I go on?" or "Where should I go first?" My answer to these is straightforward: all the adventures you want, and anywhere you please!

Dr. Robert Walker

Fostering Growth in Young Age

Picture this: growing up in Albany, GA, where the most prominent adventure might be finding a new spot that your parents would approve of you going to. The move from Camilla, a small town with fewer sidewalks than opportunities, to Albany was my first actual "travel." Though not across continents, it flipped my world upside down, peeling my eyes wide open to the sheer variety within my own backyard. It taught me that adventure doesn't need a passport; it just needs curiosity.

First up, there's this fascinating nugget from the realm of science: kids who explore new places and cultures are like sponges soaking up water—they're in the prime time of their lives for learning and absorbing new information.

Dr. P. Murali Doraiswamy, a brain health expert, points out

that novel experiences strengthen children's brain networks by forcing them to process unfamiliar information (2). This can lead to sharper minds and more creativity. Imagine your brain is a muscle; travel is the gym where it gets buff.

Then there's empathy, our mental superpower. When your kid sees that not everyone lives like they do or eats what they eat (yes, there's a whole world beyond chicken nuggets), they start to understand and appreciate diversity. That's where the real growth begins.

Children learn to communicate with people from different backgrounds, navigate unfamiliar environments, and adapt to other customs. Along the way, they also develop a sense of independence and self-confidence as they realize their own abilities and strengths.

Here's an example for you. Think of a child who has never left their home country before. They may have preconceived notions about certain cultures or countries based on what they've heard or seen in the media. But when they actually travel and experience these places for themselves, those biases are challenged and often break down completely. This is how travel nurtures open-mindedness and expands our worldview.

Now, imagine your child coming back from a trip with stories of new friends, different cultures and traditions, and a newfound understanding of the world. Not only will they have grown as individuals, but they'll also bring back valuable lessons that can shape their future in ways you may never have imagined.

So, when it comes to traveling with children, don't underestimate the impact it can have on their growth and development. Embrace their curiosity and use travel as a tool to help them become compassionate, adaptable, and open-minded individuals.

Think of travel as the most excellent, most interactive textbook you could give a child, unwrapping page by sparkly page the mysteries, stories, and wonders of this rock we call home. It's about giving them the glasses to see the world in vibrant color, the kind of learning that sticks because they've lived it, breathed it, and tasted it.

A CHILD INTO THE WORLD

The Adventure of Becoming You

An innocent family trip is flipping the script on what it means to "deal with the unexpected." Instead of a smooth experience in purchasing a second home, we faced a challenge straight out of a '90s sitcom. Finding out that a dream beach house wasn't for "our kind" wasn't just a rude awakening; it was an impromptu lesson in bouncing back with grace.

The white man, with all his rudeness and lack of hospitality, became the villain of our family story—but not the hero. Instead, my parents took it in stride and moved on to find another great place to purchase. That's when I realized they were playing the long game.

They weren't going to be bogged down by one person's bad attitude; they were going to make sure we had a great home anyway. And that's what we did.

Looking back, I see how that experience shaped my own resilience and taught me not to let others dictate my happiness or self-worth. It was a lesson in perseverance and staying true to yourself despite the challenges life may throw your way.

This wasn't just about learning to take hits; it was a masterclass in real-time problem-solving and adaptability. The kind of stuff you can't get from a book or a classroom. It's the nitty-gritty of life, served up as we navigated through unfamiliar territory. No fluff, no filler—just raw, impactful learning.

It's in moments like these—when plans go south and the world seems upside down—that the real magic of travel shines. It forces us out of our comfort bubbles and into the rolling waves of "What now?"

Travel is the ultimate teacher. It shoves us into the deep end and hollers, "Swim!" But here's the kicker: it's not about avoiding the water; it's about learning to ride the waves. When kids face challenges in unfamiliar settings—be it a language barrier or a cultural faux pas—they aren't just finding solutions.

They're building a mental toolbox brimming with creativity,

empathy, and the guts to face the unknown. This isn't about ticking boxes on a travel itinerary. It's about crafting resilient, confident souls ready to tackle life's hurdles.

Take, for instance, a family trek through the winding paths of a national park. Navigation blunders? Check. Misunderstood local customs? Double-check. Each stumble, each misstep, is a lesson in disguise. By the end of it, those kids aren't just tired hikers; they're problem-solvers equipped with a newfound understanding of the world and their place within it. It's the stuff of legend, seeing them strategize, compromise, and emerge victorious, one pint-sized step at a time.

Now, back to our beach house saga. Facing discrimination could've been a vacation ruiner. Instead, it became a teachable moment on resilience, dignity, and the power of staying true to oneself. It underscored a vital lesson: the world isn't always fair, but we have the power to choose our response. By choosing to react with integrity and strength, my parents gifted me with a lesson far beyond any textbook or classroom.

Travel doesn't just broaden horizons; it builds character. Each trip, each challenge, each triumph knits together a tapestry of experiences that shape young travelers into adaptable, confident individuals. It's a wild, excellent adventure—not just in discovering new places but in uncovering the boundless potential within each child.

Dr. Robert Walker

Chapter 2
Crafting the Ideal Itinerary for Little Feet

The very act of traveling with children is an open door to both the world's vastness and its intimate corners. This isn't just a hypothesis; it's supported by a plethora of educational theories and psychological research. Imagine a world where every street corner turns into a lesson in history, every unfamiliar dish a lesson in cultural appreciation, and every new greeting a lesson in linguistics.

Your itinerary should be a flexible blueprint, adaptive enough to cater to spontaneous curiosity while structured enough to ensure you don't miss the must-sees. Think of it as creating a playlist for your favorite road trip – each destination is a track selected not just for its rhythm but for its ability to resonate with your soul or, in this case, your family's collective heart.

In this chapter, we will discuss the key elements to consider when crafting an itinerary for Little Feet. From choosing destinations and modes of transportation to creating a balance between education and relaxation, we will cover it all.

Choosing Child-Centric Destinations

When we talk about crafting the ideal itinerary for little feet, selecting suitable destinations is like choosing the right soil for a young sapling. It's not just about the nutrients; it's about the environment that allows it to grow, thrive, and blossom. For our young explorers, every destination holds the potential to either spark a lifelong passion or teach a valuable lesson.

Why Some Places Mesmerize Young Minds More Than Others

It's simple. Kids love stories. Places rich in history, mythologies, and natural wonders speak to them in a language they understand best. Think about the ancient ruins of Rome or the vast, starlit skies of a desert camp in New Mexico. These aren't just travel spots; they're gateways to immense storybooks that children can walk through.

Dr. John Medina, a developmental molecular biologist, emphasizes how stories enhance memory retention in children (3). Apply this concept to travel, and you will witness your child remembering the trip to Rome not just as a holiday but as the day they stood where gladiators once fought.

The key here is to choose places that not only entertain but also engage. Museums like the Smithsonian in Washington, D.C., offer hands-on exhibits designed with curious minds in mind. Interactive science centers, zoos with educational programs, and national parks with junior ranger activities turn the world into a classroom where lessons are learned through experience, not lectures.

Integrating Educational Opportunities with Entertainment

This balance is crucial. It's what turns a good trip into an unforgettable adventure. Destinations should offer a mix of learning and leisure. For instance, a visit to the Kennedy Space

Center in Florida allows children to marvel at space shuttles and maybe even meet an astronaut, blending entertainment with education in a powerful way. Similarly, exploring the geological wonders of the Grand Canyon can be complemented with a fun mule ride down the steep paths, making geology more interesting than any textbook could.

In selecting locations, look for places that offer a variety of activities. This ensures that the itinerary keeps everyone's interest piqued. For example, cities like San Francisco, with its Exploratorium, or Boston, with its Freedom Trail, offer diverse experiences that cater to different ages and interests.

The Balance Between Adventure and Safety in Selecting Locations

Safety is paramount. Yet, adventure is essential for growth. The trick lies in finding destinations that offer both. This means doing your homework. Look for family-friendly accommodations, read reviews from other traveling families, and check for safe public transportation options. Places like Orlando, Florida, not only boast theme parks like Disney World but also have a well-structured city layout that's friendly for visitors and families.

Places like the Rocky Mountain National Park in Colorado offer a safe yet adventurous experience. Well-marked trails, ranger-led programs, and family-friendly facilities ensure safety while allowing children to explore nature's wonders.

In conclusion, choosing child-centric destinations is about creating memories that enrich the soul and spark curiosity. It's about watching your child's eyes light up as they discover the world's wonders. With each destination, we're not just traveling. We're cultivating little minds to become the globe-trotters of tomorrow.

Dr. Robert Walker

Interactive Itineraries

Creating an itinerary that captivates and engages your children requires more than just penciling in visits to the most popular attractions. It's about weaving their interests, energy levels, and curiosity into the very fabric of your travel plans. This approach ensures that every day of your trip is not just an adventure but a cherished memory in the making.

Designing a Kid-Approved Agenda That Involves Their Input

Getting your kids involved in the planning process can be a game-changer. Think of it like building a Lego set. You have the instructions (your travel plans) and the bricks (the destinations and activities). But it's the imagination and enthusiasm of your little ones that will decide what you're building together.

Start simple. Show them pictures or videos of the destinations and ask what they find exciting. Younger children might be fascinated by the idea of seeing animals in the wild, while older kids might be intrigued by historical sites or space centers. This process not only makes the trip more engaging for them but also teaches valuable lessons in decision-making

Dr. Robert Walker

Structuring Days with Flexibility, Incorporating Both High-Energy Activities and Rest

Balance is key. Every itinerary should have a rhythm, like a well-curated playlist that has both upbeat tunes for dancing and slower songs for winding down. Planning days with a mix of high-energy activities and relaxed downtime caters to the natural ebbs and flows of your child's enthusiasm and stamina. For instance, a morning spent exploring the ruins of an ancient castle could be followed by an afternoon at a quiet beach or park. This paced approach prevents burnout and keeps spirits high throughout the trip.

Making Room for Spontaneous Exploration Alongside Planned Visits

Sometimes, the best memories come from unexpected adventures. Leave gaps in your schedule for spontaneous exploration. This could mean wandering down a side street to discover a local market or deciding on a whim to join a street art tour.

Such experiences enrich your travel tapestry with vibrant, unscripted moments that often become the most talked-about stories of your trip. Remember, the goal is to create a blend of structured and free-flow adventures that cater to your family's interests and energy levels.

Traveling with children is not just about seeing new places; it's about experiencing them together, through their eyes and with their sense of wonder. An interactive itinerary doesn't bind you to a checklist; instead, it serves as a flexible guide tailored to your family's unique rhythm and interests, making each trip an unforgettable chapter in your collective story.

Safety Through Preparation

Traveling ignites curiosity and wonder in children, an invaluable gift from parents. But ensuring their safety is paramount. It's like launching a space shuttle. Every detail matters. The plan must be foolproof. Here, we'll explore the

A CHILD INTO THE WORLD

nitty-gritty of keeping your little astronauts secure on this earthly expedition.

Tools and Practices for Security in Unfamiliar Environments

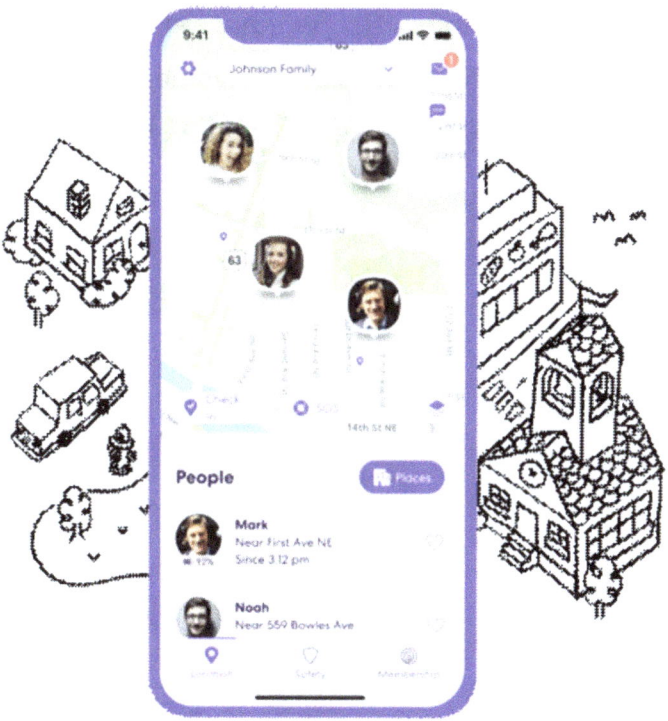

It starts with the basics. Always have both digital and physical copies of your child's identification. In the digital age, apps like Find My Friends or Life360 can be lifesavers, allowing real-time location tracking. But technology can fail, which is why the old-school method of a waterproof wristband with your contact details still holds value.

Teach your children about safety in a way that doesn't scare them but empowers them. Use simple language to explain what to do if they get lost. Have a clear plan—choose a recognizable landmark as a meeting point whenever you're in crowded places, and practice this plan.

Remember, your child watches how you interact with the world. Demonstrating cautious engagement with strangers teaches them to do the same. It's about striking a balance: encourage curiosity, but instill a sense of caution.

Preparing for Common Travel Mishaps with a Child-Centered Approach

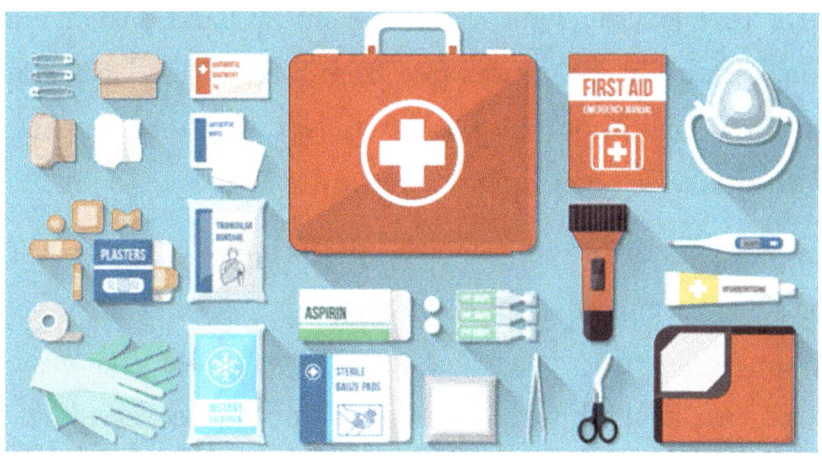

Mishaps can be teaching moments. Lost luggage? It's an opportunity to show resilience and improvisation by making a game out of wearing the same superhero shirt two days in a row. Delayed flights? Explore the airport as if it's a jungle, hunting for hidden treasures (aka snacks or play areas).

Keep a small medical kit tailored to your child's needs. Include not just the essentials like band-aids and antiseptics, but also a few comforts from home, whether that's a specific snack or their favorite toy.

Also, prepare for dietary mishaps. Research local food options. If your child has specific needs or allergies, equip yourself with local phrases that can help communicate these to servers or hosts. Tools like Google Translate can be a game-changer here, turning potential stress into a smooth dining experience.

Safe travels are joyful travels. Your preparations lay the foundation for adventures free from worry. This isn't about shielding them from the world but preparing them to meet it with eyes wide open and minds ready to learn.

Every safety tip or tool you employ is a stepping stone toward building confident, world-savvy children. You're not just planning a trip; you're crafting experiences that teach resilience, adaptability, and the sheer joy of discovery.

In the grand architecture of childhood, every travel experience is a brick. Safety is the mortar. Together, they build a resilient, curious, and joyful adult.

Chapter 3
Education on the Go

When children step into new cultures, they're not just tourists—they're young anthropologists, keenly observing and absorbing. Every marketplace is a lesson in economics; every natural landscape is a class in environmental science.

But how exactly does this work? Research shows that kids who travel score higher on academic measures (4). It's not just about the places they see but the skills they develop. Navigation boosts spatial awareness. Ordering food in a foreign language sharpens cognitive abilities. Even the act of packing ingrains organizational skills. Travel teaches resilience, problem-solving, and adaptability—skills highly prized in today's rapidly changing world.

Consider this: A child visiting historical sites develops a deeper understanding and interest in history, surpassing any textbook description. A trip to a science museum in another country can spark an interest in technology and innovation.

Now, I know what you're thinking: "This sounds amazing, but how do I ensure it's educational and not just leisure?" The secret lies in engagement. Before the trip, involve your children in the planning. Research destinations together. Discuss the history and culture of the places you'll visit. This pre-trip involvement boosts anticipation and investment in learning.

Education on the go is akin to baking a perfect cake. You need the right ingredients (destinations), the correct measurements (planning and balancing leisure and learning), and the ideal temperature (engagement and enthusiasm). Miss one, and your cake falls flat. Nail them all, and you create something both delicious and memorable.

In the following pages, we'll guide you through crafting educational journeys—filled with specific tips, tools, and tales—that bring learning to life. From navigating the logistics of educational travel to ensuring the experiences are as enriching as they are enjoyable, we've got you covered.

A CHILD INTO THE WORLD

Real-World Learning Unleashed

Travel thrusts children into a live, interactive learning environment. It's where the rubber meets the road in education. Think of it as the ultimate classroom without walls. Here, experiences are the teachers, and every destination is a textbook filled with lessons waiting to be discovered.

Dr. Robert Walker

Experiential Learning

Imagine learning about marine life by snorkeling in the Great Barrier Reef rather than flipping through a textbook's pages. The vivid colors, the feel of the water, and the live ecosystem create a memorable learning experience etched in the child's memory. Why does this work so well?

Science tells us that experiential learning—the process of learning through experience—is far more effective than rote memorization. It engages all the senses, making the lesson unforgettable. Children remember 90% of what they do compared to just 10% of what they read. This isn't just education; it's an adventure that educates.

A CHILD INTO THE WORLD

Enhancing Problem-Solving and Adaptability

Travel puts children in situations where they must adapt antime time time time time real-time. Lost luggage? That's a lesson in dealing with unexpected challenges. A missed train? Here comes a crash course in scheduling and time management. These aren't merely inconveniences; they're opportunities in disguise.

Each challenge faced and solved reinforces the child's ability to adapt and think critically. This is the sort of soft skill that will be highly valued in the workforce in the future. It's about preparing them not just academically but for life.

The concept of Zone of Proximal Development (ZPD) suggests

that children learn best when they are guided through tasks slightly beyond their comfort zone yet within their capability to achieve with support (5). Travel naturally creates this environment. Navigating new cities, learning a few phrases in a different language, or understanding cultural norms—these experiences push children just enough to expand their boundaries. With each trip, their ZPD expands, making way for new skills and knowledge.

It's not just about seeing new places but about transforming how we view learning and development. Travel is the bridge connecting theoretical knowledge with real-world application. It turns abstract concepts into concrete understanding.

A CHILD INTO THE WORLD

The Tapestry of Cultures

Think of culture as a vast, intricate quilt. Each piece, sewn with care, tells its own story—a story infused with traditions, beliefs, and values. Now imagine wrapping your child in this quilt. Not only does it keep them warm, but with each thread, it imparts wisdom. This is what cultural immersion does: it wraps children in a layer of understanding and connection that goes beyond mere observation.

When families travel, they don't just see landmarks; they feel the pulse of the culture. Consider this: a visit to a local market in Marrakech offers more than souvenirs. It's a live lesson in economics, trade, negotiation, and human interaction. Children learn the value of money, the art of bargaining, and perhaps most importantly, the importance of respecting different ways of life. This interaction isn't just educational; it's the groundwork for empathy and global citizenship.

Imagine your child sitting down to a meal with a local family. They may notice differences in dining etiquette or meal timings. Yet, as they break bread together, they see the universal language of hospitality and kindness. This lesson in cultural norms and shared humanity is powerful.

Research shows that children who engage in such profound cultural experiences display heightened empathy, more vital interpersonal skills, and a broader understanding of the world (6). Simply, these experiences mold them into well-rounded individuals.

Curating Authentic Experiences

It's not enough to travel. To truly weave the cultural tapestry into our children's hearts, we must curate authentic experiences. This means going beyond the hotel and guided tours. It means connecting with local families, participating in traditional activities, and, yes, sometimes, getting wonderfully lost. In doing so, we gift our children a profound understanding and appreciation of diversity.

The beauty of this approach? It ties back to everything we've discussed earlier. Just as learning through travel empowers children with adaptability and problem-solving, cultural immersion shapes them into compassionate global citizens.

Each trip, each interaction, adds another colorful thread to their quilt. It's a practical application of educational theories—bringing concepts of empathy, adaptability, and global awareness from the abstract into the tangible.

Practical Language Adventures

When you travel with kids, language barriers become opportunities, not obstacles. Think of it like unlocking a new level in a video game—the challenge is part of the fun, and success brings incredible rewards. Language is the key to unlocking a country's culture. It's about more than just words; it's about connection.

Before you go, get familiar. Learn "hello," "thank you," and "help" in the local language. It's like rolling out a welcome mat for yourselves. Kids pick up languages fast. Encourage them to use these words. Each time they do, it's a mini-win. Celebrate it. These aren't just words; they're open doors.

Language games are gold. Create a bingo card with local words. Each time they hear or use one, they get to mark it off. The first one to get five in a row wins a prize. The prize? Make it local. Maybe it's a treat from a nearby bakery. The goal is to make learning fun and rewarding.

Every interaction is a lesson. Ordering food? Have them do it. Buying a ticket? They can ask. It's practice in action. This isn't just about language; it's about courage and independence. They're not just learning words; they're learning to navigate the world.

This approach is backed by the principle of immersive learning. It's proven. When you're in it, you learn faster. You remember more. This isn't just language learning; it's brain-building.

To wrap it up, think of language as a magic wand. It turns strangers into friends. It transforms watching into experiencing. As you travel, wield this wand and watch the world open up.

A CHILD INTO THE WORLD

Making History Accessible

Imagine stepping back in time with your child, where history is not just a story from a book but a vivid, tangible world they can explore and interact with. This is the power of travel in educating young ones—it makes history come alive.

Take, for example, the ancient Colosseum in Rome. Instead of reading about gladiators, your child stands in the very arena where they once battled. This experience cements historical facts in their mind in a way a classroom lesson never could. It's immersive learning at its best.

When you visit a historical landmark, talk about who walked those grounds before you. Discuss what life was like in that era. Make it a game to find the oldest artifact or to imagine what a day in the life of a historical figure would have been like. These activities don't just teach history; they spark curiosity. Curiosity leads to questions. Questions seek answers. This cycle is the essence of learning.

Storytelling is another powerful tool. Every historic site has a story. Before visiting, read these stories together. Then, standing before these landmarks, recount the tales. This method helps to frame their visit, giving context to what they see. For younger children, encourage them to draw what they imagine the story looked like. Ask older kids to write a short story or diary entry from the perspective of someone living in that time.

Hands-on activities can range from participating in a medieval fair to crafting an ancient tool or cooking a historical dish. These experiences are not just fun—they're educational. They provide a tactile connection to history, making abstract concepts concrete.

Linking back to language learning from our previous section, imagine visiting Japan and learning about the Samurai warriors. Your child learns historical terms in Japanese, connecting the language to its cultural roots. This deepens their understanding and appreciation for both the language and the history.

Understanding history plays a crucial role in shaping compassionate global citizens. It teaches empathy, perspective, and critical thinking. When children learn history by being "in it," they understand the complexities of human nature and culture. They see the consequences of actions and decisions. They know that their actions today can shape the future.

To wrap it up, think of travel as a time machine. It transforms the abstract into the concrete. It turns history lessons into adventures. This method of learning sticks. It inspires. Most importantly, it prepares our children to be thoughtful, informed citizens of the world. And isn't that what education is all about?

Travel is like the course of a river. Its continuous flow shapes the landscape, just as immersive history lessons shape a child's understanding and perspective. Keep the narrative engaging. Offer specifics, like visiting the Great Wall of China and counting the steps they climb or guessing how many bricks it took to build it.

Dr. Robert Walker

Chapter 4
Budget Travelling with Children

Travel Smarter, Not Harder. That's our motto. Picture this - a family vacation where every dollar stretches like the endless horizon you're exploring together. It's possible. How? Strategic planning and a dash of creativity. We're talking about early bird specials that are kinder to your wallet, accommodations that offer a genuine taste of local life, and activities that are enriching, educational, and economically savvy.

Here's a little secret – children don't tally up the cost of experiences; they soak up the joy. Whether it's a $10 hands-on cooking class in a small Italian village or a free day exploring ancient ruins, what they'll remember is the thrill of discovery.

Let's get down to brass tacks with **specific tips and numbers**. Did you know booking your flights on a Tuesday can save you an average of 10% compared to weekend prices? Or can family memberships to global science centers or museums cost less than three separate visits, offering endless learning opportunities in cities around the world? These aren't just numbers; they're your tools for unlocking an affordable globe-trotting experience.

Imagine teaching your children the value of money and budgeting, not through lectures but through the exciting world of travel. It's like a live-action game of Monopoly, but instead of buying properties, you're collecting priceless moments.

We'll explore psychological insights, showing how experiences, not possessions, are the true builders of happiness and contentment. Business psychology tells us that consumers find more lasting satisfaction in experiences. Apply this to family travel, and you're investing in a lifetime of joy and shared memories.

By the end of this chapter, you'll view budget constraints not as barriers but as creative challenges. With each tip and trick, you are one step closer to becoming a travel-savvy parent, capable of whisking your family away on enriching adventures without the sting of financial stress. This isn't just travel; it's a masterclass in life lessons for you and your children, served up with a side of joy and a sprinkle of adventure.

Dr. Robert Walker

Smart Savings Secrets

When planning a family vacation, think of your budget as a compass. It guides you but doesn't limit where you can go. Imagine the world as a giant theme park. Some attractions have fast lanes that cost a bit more. Others are free but just as thrilling. This is your adventure map to those hidden gems.

First up, timing is everything. Booking flights and accommodations early can save you a fortune. Airlines release tickets at their lowest prices about six months in advance. Grabbing these deals can cut flight costs significantly. For hotels, booking three to four months ahead often secures the best rates.

Consider this: A family of four traveling to Paris might spend $1,500 on flights if booked at the last minute. Plan and book six months prior? That could drop to $900. You've just saved $600. That's a whole lot of croissants and museum entries.

Travel during the off-peak season. Prices plummet, crowds dissipate, and the experience remains unforgettable. Schools have breaks at different times. Use this to your advantage. A ski trip in late March or a beach holiday in early June can halve your expenses compared to peak times.

Imagine skiing down less crowded slopes or enjoying a serene beach sunset. These moments don't cost extra; they're priceless. Yet, you've paid much less for them.

Rewards Programs and Memberships

Loyalty pays. Sign up for airline rewards programs. Collect points on everyday purchases. Then, use them to book flights or upgrades. Many programs are free. They offer benefits beyond flights, like discounts on car rentals and hotels.

Here's a real gem. Family memberships to global attractions offer unlimited visits. The New York Museum of Science might have a reciprocal agreement with London's Science Museum. One membership, multiple cities, endless exploration. Plus, these memberships often come with additional perks like discounts at the gift shop or cafe.

Dr. Robert Walker

Living Like a Local

Forget pricey hotels. Think vacation rentals or home swaps. Platforms like Airbnb offer the chance to stay in unique places. They're often cheaper and more spacious. Plus, having a kitchen saves a fortune on dining out.

Some families save up to 50% on accommodation by choosing rentals over hotels. Imagine staying in a cozy apartment in Rome for half the price of a hotel. That's more money for gelato and experiencing local life.

Eating out is part of the fun, but it can drain your budget. Mix things up. Visit local markets, cook meals, and have picnics. This not only saves money but also turns mealtime into an adventure.

Consider this: Eating out in Tokyo might cost $40 per person. A visit to a local market? You could have a feast for under $20 for the whole family. Plus, it's a culinary adventure, exploring new foods and flavors.

Intelligent savings aren't about cutting corners; they're about making smart choices that enhance your travel experience. It's finding joy in the simple things. Remember, the most significant expense is missing out on the adventure. And adventure doesn't have to cost a lot. Your family memories are waiting to be made affordably.

A CHILD INTO THE WORLD

Hidden Gem Destinations

Remember the lessons from earlier about intelligent savings? The same applies when seeking out hidden gem destinations with your family. Think of these lesser-known spots as off-the-beaten-path playgrounds for budget-savvy travelers. These are places where the adventure is rich, but the cost is not.

One such place is the natural beauty of Utah's national parks. Zion and Bryce Canyon offer breathtaking landscapes at a fraction of the cost of more famous parks. A family pass costs less than $80 for a week. This is where your children can learn geology by walking through it rather than reading from a book.

Less crowded than Disney World and cheaper, too. Here's the kicker: Lodging nearby is affordable. A family can stay for less than $100 a night during off-peak seasons. Compare that to the average $200-plus for accommodations near major theme parks.

Moving towards the coast, consider the hidden beaches of the Oregon Coast. Unlike its Californian counterpart, Oregon's coastline offers rugged beauty without the hefty price tag. Think sea stacks and tide pools teeming with life. It's a biology lesson waiting to happen.

Here's the science bit: Business psychology suggests that experiences, especially novel ones, enhance our happiness more than material goods. These hidden gems provide unique experiences that stick. They're the stories your family will tell for years.

A week-long stay in a quaint beachside town in Oregon can be less than $700 in a vacation rental, with ocean views. Dining out? Seafood caught that day for less than $30 for a family meal. Unforgettable memories? Priceless.

Don't overlook the Midwest's charm. South Dakota's Black Hills pack a massive punch. Here lies Mount Rushmore, yes, but also Custer State Park, where bison roam free. It's a safari without airfare to Africa. Here, the nightly rates for a family cabin start at around $150.

Outdoor adventures abound. Think horseback riding or hiking among the peaks and pines. This isn't just a holiday; it's an immersive experience in American history and nature. It's far cheaper than a theme park adventure and far richer in content.

Tying all this back to our intelligent savings talk: Choosing destinations like these means your budget stretches further. You can afford more adventures. More importantly, you gift your children experiences that shape their view of the world—experiences that teach more than any classroom could.

Innovative Entertainment on a Budget

It's not just about the destinations but the experiences along the way. This is where innovative entertainment comes in. It's about being savvy—making the most of what's around you. It doesn't have to cost much, if anything at all.

Free Local Events – Every city has free events. These can range from museum days to outdoor concerts. It's like a treasure hunt. Find these events; they provide rich experiences. A concert under the stars. A street fair. These moments become the highlights of your trip. And the cost? Zero.

Nature's Playground – The great outdoors is free. National parks offer fee-free days. Plan around these. A hike. A day by the lake. These are the backdrops for family adventures. It's not just fun; it's educational. Children learn about geology and ecology. They see it. They touch it. They remember it.

DIY Entertainment Packs – Think outside the toy box. Create your own entertainment packs: scavenger hunts, travel journals. These keep kids engaged. They're learning, observing, writing. And you? You're saving. No need for expensive gadgets. The best part? These packs can change. Tailor them to each destination.

Remember, the goal is creating memories. It's like knitting. Each stitch is a moment. Together, they form a tapestry of experiences—rich, colorful, priceless.

Studies show that experiences contribute more to our happiness than material goods (7). This isn't just talk; it's science. Experiencing new places, events, and activities with your family? It's gold—emotional gold. It strengthens bonds. It broadens horizons.

Traveling on a budget doesn't mean skimping on the fun. It's about smart choices—choices that enrich your family's experience. Choices that turn simple moments into lasting memories. And the cost? Minimal. The value? Immense. It's an investment in your family's happiness. An investment in your children's education about the world.

Dr. Robert Walker

Chapter 5
Packing Tips and Tricks

Imagine this: the light breeze of anticipation before a family trip, where each item packed is a pixel in the big picture of your adventure. This chapter isn't just about what socks or which toothbrush to bring. It's about transforming packing from a dreaded chore into the first step of your travel tale.

Packing smarter, not harder; that's what we're after. Ever heard of the psychological concept called "decision fatigue"? It's real, and it affects us all, especially when we are packing. The idea is simple—the more choices we face, the quicker we tire, making each subsequent decision more daunting than the last. I'll show you how to streamline your decision-making, making packing a breeze.

Here's the deal: I'm not just throwing ideas into the wind. The strategies shared here are backed by hours of research and personal experimentation. They're your ticket to leaving behind the anxiety of forgotten toothpaste or the classic "I packed too much" dilemma.

A specific tip? Roll your clothes instead of folding them. It saves space and reduces wrinkles. Numbers don't lie—rolling can free up to 30% more space. That's a whole third of your suitcase for souvenirs or those extra shoes you debated bringing.

But here's a curveball: packing also teaches prioritization and restraint, invaluable skills in both travel and life. Think of your suitcase as a miniaturized version of your life. Only so much fits, so what do you value the most?

In essence, this chapter is designed to equip you with knowledge, skills, and a hefty dose of confidence. Confidence that you're packing precisely what your family needs—nothing more, nothing less. By the end, you'll look at a suitcase and see not a challenge but a canvas, ready to be filled with the essentials for your next grand adventure.

Dr. Robert Walker

Interactive Packing Checklists

PACKING LIST

DESTINATION(S) Dominican Republic   DATE(S) May 5-12th, 2020   NUMBER OF DAYS 8

ESSENTIALS
- ☐ Driver's license/ID
- ☐ Passport
- ☐ Visa
- ☐ Medications
- ☐ Money/Wallet
- ☐ Tickets
- ☐ Travel itinerary
- ☐ Credit/debit cards
- ☐ Contacts list
- ☐ Directions
- ☐
- ☐

TRIP PLANNING
- ☐ Guide Book(s)
- ☐ Hotel information
- ☐ Pens
- ☐ Journal/Diary
- ☐
- ☐
- ☐

ACCESSORIES
- ☐ Jewelry
- ☐ Day bag/purse
- ☐ Evening bag/purse
- ☐ Belt
- ☐ Hats
- ☐
- ☐

TOILETRIES
- ☐ Sunscreen
- ☐ Mosquito repellant
- ☐ Toothpaste
- ☐ Toothbrush
- ☐ Tampons/sanitary pads

CLOTHING
- ☐ Jeans/pants - 6
- ☐ Leggings - 2
- ☐ Skirts - 2
- ☐ Dresses - 2
- ☐ Short sleeve tops - 4
- ☐ Dressy shirts - 2
- ☐ T-shirts - 4
- ☐ Gray cardigan
- ☐ Tank top - 3
- ☐
- ☐
- ☐

OUTERWEAR
- ☐ Jacket/Windbreaker
- ☐ Hat
- ☐ Gloves
- ☐ Scarf
- ☐ Snow pants
- ☐ Long johns
- ☐ Ski/snowboard gear

BEACHWEAR
- ☐ Swimsuit
- ☐ Hat
- ☐ Cover-up/Sarong
- ☐ Sunglasses
- ☐ Beach tote
- ☐
- ☐

- ☐ Adhesive bandages
- ☐ Shampoo
- ☐ Conditioner
- ☐ Soap/Body wash
- ☐ Styling products

SHOES
- ☐ Long sleeve shirts - 2
- ☐ Sweaters - 1
- ☐ Shorts - 2
- ☐ Capris
- ☐ Tights
- ☐ Belt
- ☐ Workout clothes

MAKE-UP
- ☐ Facial moisturizer
- ☐ Face make-up
- ☐ Concealer
- ☐ Mascara
- ☐ Eye shadow
- ☐ Eye liner
- ☐ Blush
- ☐ Lipstick
- ☐ Lip balm
- ☐ Makeup remover
- ☐ Perfume
- ☐ Night cream
- ☐ Facial scrub

PACKING
- ☐ Toiletries bag
- ☐ Money belt
- ☐ Laundry bag
- ☐ Makeup bag
- ☐ Airline liquids bags

SHOES
- ☐ Sneakers/tennis shoes
- ☐ Walking shoes
- ☐ Sandals
- ☐ Flip-flops
- ☐ Black heels
- ☐ Brown heels
- ☐ Boots

UNDERWEAR
- ☐ Panties
- ☐ Bras
- ☐ Socks
- ☐ Pajamas tops - 3
- ☐ Pajama bottoms - 3
- ☐ Nightgown

BUSINESS
- ☐ Suits
- ☐ Ties
- ☐ Presentation materials
- ☐ Note pads
- ☐ Business cards

ELECTRONICS
- ☐ Phone and charger
- ☐ Tablet and charger
- ☐ eReader and charger
- ☐ Headphones
- ☐ Laptop and charger

Packing can be chaos. Clothes everywhere. Forgot your toothbrush? Typical. But here's a game changer - **Interactive Packing Checklists**. Think of it like a treasure hunt. Each item on the list is a treasure to be found and packed. This isn't just about remembering socks. It's about turning packing into a fun, engaging activity for your kids.

Interaction is key. Kids love feeling included. Giving them their own checklist does just that. It's like a mission—they're in charge of their stuff. This teaches responsibility. They learn what they need and understand that packing isn't just throwing things in a bag. It's selecting what matters.

The psychology behind this? Ownership. When kids choose and check off their items, they take ownership. This reduces anxiety. They feel prepared. And it saves time—no more last-minute rushes to pack their favorite toy.

Here's how you do it: Create a list for your child. Include pictures for younger kids. Each item they pack, they tick off. Make it colorful, bold, and use fun fonts. Add rewards, like, "Pack all your items, and we'll pick a special travel snack." This turns a mundane task into an adventure.

Remember, the goal is to simplify not just for you but for them. This approach makes the process manageable. They won't overpack. They learn to prioritize. Just like in life, not everything can come along. They pick what's essential and see the result—a well-packed bag with everything they need.

This ties perfectly with our earlier point on efficient packing. It's all about bringing what you need, no extras. This method encourages that and provides a practical lesson in minimalism—in a fun, engaging way.

Dr. Robert Walker

The Travel Journal Kit

A journal is more than a book. It's a vault for memories, ideas, and reflections. Picture this: Your child, armed with a journal, becomes a young explorer, documenting their discoveries. Each entry helps them process what they see and feel. *Here's where it gets interesting*: The act of writing enhances observation and reflection skills. They're not just passing through the world; they're engaging with it, understanding it, and remembering it.

Your child might not remember every beach they've visited, but they will recall the story of the day they journaled about building the tallest sandcastle and the wave that toppled it over.

Engagement and learning through fun is a concept borrowed from business psychology. Gamification in the workplace boosts productivity and motivation. Applying these principles to travel prep turns tedious tasks into exciting adventures. The journal kit becomes a coveted item. Something they look forward to using each day of the trip.

Now, for the actionable part. **Here's how to assemble a practical Travel Journal Kit** -

1. **The Journal** - Opt for durable, age-appropriate notebooks. Include stickers or stamps for added fun.

2. **Colors Galore** - Pack colored pens, pencils, and even watercolors. Visual memory is potent. The more vivid the entry, the stronger the memory.

3. **Guidance** - Initially, guide them. Suggest topics to write about. What was the funniest thing that happened today? What new food did you try? This encourages them to observe and engage.

Incorporate the Travel Journal Kit into the packing process. Make it a reward for completing their packing checklist. It's like hitting two birds with one stone. They're thrilled to complete their packing. And they're eager to start journaling.

The Travel Journal Kit does more than keep your kids busy. It helps them grow. They become more attentive, reflective, and expressive. They learn to see more than just sights. They learn to see stories. Experiences. Lessons. All tucked neatly into their backpacks, ready to be discovered again, years down the road, through the pages of their travel journals.

Dr. Robert Walker

The Essential Emergency Kit

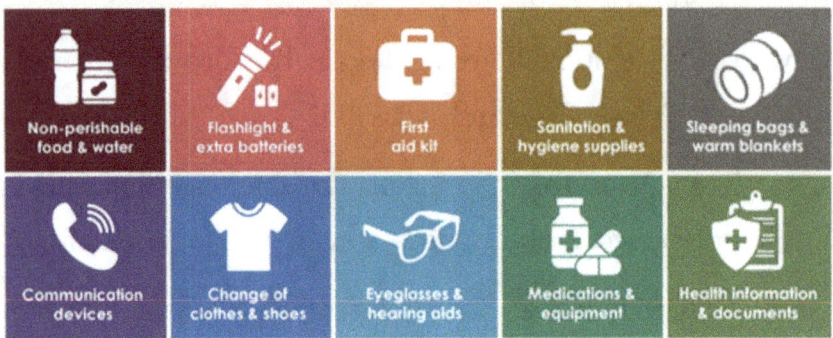

First Things First, Safety. Imagine this. Your child scrapes their knee while exploring a medieval castle in Europe or develops a slight fever under the tropical sun. Is the adventure you planned suitable? But with an Emergency Kit at hand, you quickly transition from a worried parent to a superhero. **It's all about being prepared.** This kit isn't just a collection of items; it's your first line of defense, ensuring minor mishaps don't turn into major spoilers.

Packing the Perfect Kit - Here's where specifics matter. Your kit should include -

- **Band-aids -** For those unexpected scrapes and cuts.
- **Antiseptic wipes -** To clean wounds effectively.
- **Over-the-counter pain relievers -** Like acetaminophen or ibuprofen, for sudden pains or fevers.

- **Tweezers** - For splinter removal.
- **Rehydration salts** - To combat dehydration, especially after long walks or if someone falls ill.
- **Thermometer** - Knowing if it's a fever or just fatigue can make all the difference.
- **Allergy medication** - Because you never know when a new food might trigger a reaction.

This preparedness mirrors life's more significant lessons of responsibility and foresight. Just as we instill the importance of packing their own bag in children, teaching them the significance of safety through the Emergency Kit is equally vital. They learn, through observation and involvement, the necessity of being ready for the unexpected.

While the Travel Journal Kit captures the essence of experiences, the Emergency Kit safeguards the continuation of these adventures. Together, they form the perfect companions for any trip, ensuring not only the enrichment of the mind but also the well-being of the body.

Think of it as packing a parachute when boarding a plane; you hope never to use it, but its presence is reassuring. ***Happy travels mean prepared travels***. With this guide, you're not just packing; you're preparing for a seamless experience filled with joy, learning, and, most importantly, safety.

Dr. Robert Walker

Packing teaches something adults know all too well: preparing for the future can be half the fun. For the child, the Travel Journal Kit and the Essential Emergency Kit become tangible representations of this idea. And with each trip, these kits continue to evolve, just like our little travelers themselves.

A CHILD INTO THE WORLD

Chapter 6
Navigating Travel Challenges

Travel, especially with children, is akin to a thrilling roller coaster ride. It's filled with ups, downs, and unexpected turns. **Picture this:** You're all set for your family adventure—bags packed, kids buzzing with excitement—and bam! You encounter your first hiccup. Maybe it's a missed connection, a lost suitcase, or a sudden bout of the flu. These moments might feel daunting, especially when you're far from home and comfort. But **here's the twist:** it's these very challenges that can transform a simple vacation into an epic family saga.

The beauty of travel isn't found in the perfect moments. It's hidden in the imperfections. The delays, detours, and roadblocks teach resilience, flexibility, and problem-solving—skills that are invaluable, not just on the road, but in life.

In this chapter, we'll tackle the unpredictable with strategies that have been tested in the trenches. For instance, did you know that a study found families who encountered and overcame travel hiccups reported a higher sense of satisfaction and stronger bonding post-trip? Yes, the struggle, weirdly enough, brought joy.

We'll explore tangible, no-nonsense advice—like always packing an 'emergency' entertainment kit for sudden delays or the importance of instilling a 'team' mindset in your kids. This isn't about sugarcoating the issues; it's about preparing and powering through. Teaching your kids to adapt and thrive in the face of challenges is a gift.

A CHILD INTO THE WORLD

Transforming Jet Lag into a Journey Adjustment Tool

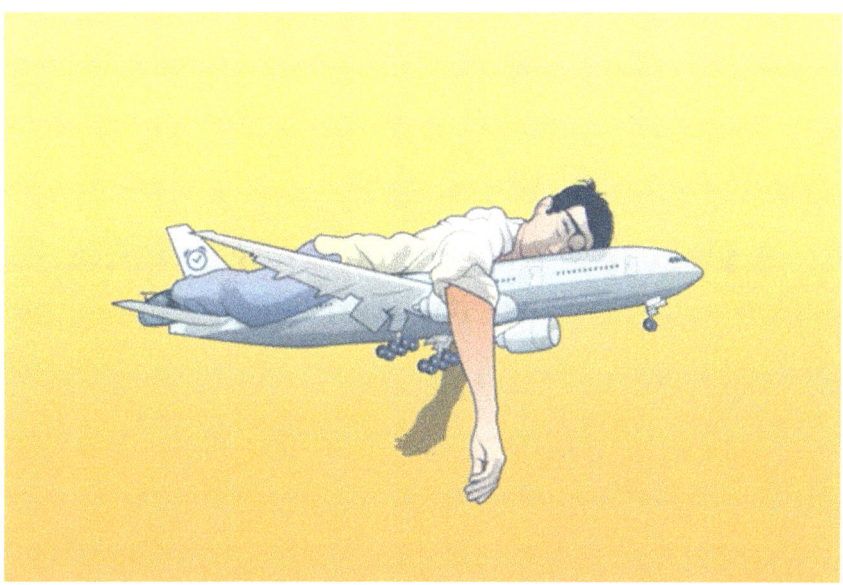

Jet lag often feels like an unwelcome guest on our travels. It sneaks up on us, disrupting our body clocks and confusing our kids. **But what if I told you that jet lag could actually be an ally?** A tool to help your children learn and adapt. It's all about perspective.

First, understand the science. Our bodies operate on a 24-hour cycle called the circadian rhythm. When we cross time zones, our internal clocks fall out of sync. **Here comes the absorbing part:** This disruption isn't just a nuisance; it's a wake-up call to our brains, urging them to adjust. And that's where the learning begins.

Consider this: Jet lag is the body's way of saying, "Hey, something new is happening." It's the perfect moment to teach your kids about time zones, geography, and the importance of flexibility. Explain to them why the sun is setting at a different time than they're used to. Make it a game: Who can adjust the fastest?

A Creative Approach to Managing Meltdowns

Traveling with children is like navigating a ship through unpredictable seas. One moment, the water is calm, and the next, you're facing a storm - the storm being meltdowns. **But fear not, parents.** We have the tools to weather these outbursts with grace and teach our kids valuable coping skills in the process.

Understand the 'Why' Behind Meltdowns

First, it's crucial to grasp *why* meltdowns happen. They're not acts of rebellion. Instead, think of meltdowns as your child's way of saying, "I can't process everything going on." It could be fatigue, hunger, or overstimulation. Recognizing the cause is step one. It's like detective work. Each clue brings you closer to preventing or mitigating the next episode.

Dr. Robert Walker

Strategies That Work

1. **Travel Timeout -** Not punishment, but a break. Find a quiet spot. Help your child breathe deeply. It calms the mind. Counting to ten together isn't just child's play; it's a proven method to reduce stress and regain control. This technique can turn a potential hour-long meltdown into a matter of minutes of reset.

2. **Meltdown Map -** Before the trip, sit down with your child. Discuss what might overwhelm them. Create a simple 'map' of these triggers. This prep work empowers them. They learn to identify and articulate their feelings before they escalate. Psychology backs this up. A study showed that children who can express

their emotions are less likely to have meltdowns. They feel understood and safe.

3. **The Power of Distraction -** Keep a small bag of new toys or books on hand. They don't need to be costly. Just new to them. The novelty is critical. It's a psychological trick. New stimuli capture their attention and distract them from the meltdown trigger. It's a simple yet effective way to redirect their focus and mood.

Consider the case of a family who reported frequent meltdowns during their travels. They started implementing these strategies, focusing on early detection and intervention. The outcome? Their trips became smoother, they enjoyed more quality time together, and their child began to look forward to travel instead of dreading it. They reported fewer meltdowns and more engagement with new experiences. This transformation is possible for your family, too.

Remember, every meltdown is an opportunity. It's a chance to teach, to bond, and to grow. With the right approach, you can turn these challenges into moments of learning and laughter. Safe travels, and may your family's journey be as smooth as your flight.

Dr. Robert Walker

Overcoming the Challenge of Lost Stuff

Losing things while traveling can feel like hitting a bump on a smooth road. It disrupts your flow. Especially with kids, it's almost a given. Toys, books, or even passports can go missing in action. **But here's the silver lining.** These moments can teach lessons in responsibility and resilience.

The Art of Preparation

Preparation is your first line of defense. Tag everything. Sounds simple, right? It is. Yet, it's incredibly effective. Use bright, distinctive tags on your luggage, backpacks, and even on your kids' favorite toys. Make these tags unique to your family. This step might seem small. However, it increases the chances of finding lost items significantly.

Remember, it's not just about preventing loss. It's about easing recovery. A study pointed out that items tagged with precise, personalized identifiers are almost 85% more likely to be returned. These stats speak volumes. They show being proactive works.

Turning Losses into Learning Opportunities

When something does go missing, don't panic. Use it as a teachable moment. Sit down with your child. Discuss what happened. Encourage them to think about where they last saw the item. This process is crucial. It builds their problem-solving skills. It's like a real-life puzzle. They learn to trace their steps. This skill is invaluable, not just in travel but in life.

The Backup Plan

Always have backups for the essentials. Think **passports**, **tickets**, and yes, even **toys**. Keep digital copies of your important documents accessible on your phone. For toys and comfort items, consider duplicates. The idea is not to overpack; it's about strategic packing. By having these backups, you ensure peace of mind and are ready for those bumps in the road.

Connecting this to the earlier conversations about meltdowns, losing a favorite toy could trigger an outburst. Here's where your backup strategy shines. It's your safety net. It allows you to handle these situations with grace and shows your kids that planning ahead can turn a potentially stressful situation into a minor hiccup.

In essence, dealing with lost items while traveling teaches critical life lessons. It's about being prepared, staying calm, and thinking clearly. These lessons are significant; they prepare your children for the unpredictable journeys of life. Just as a captain navigates through storms with preparation and skill, you're guiding your family through the adventures of travel.

Keep it fun but meaningful. That's our mantra. Travel not only broadens horizons. It strengthens character. And as we've seen, even the challenges have silver linings. They're opportunities for growth. Safe travels, and may your belongings always find their way back to you.

Navigating Missed Schedules

Missed schedules while traveling with children are inevitable. Like a domino effect, one delay can knock the entire day's plans off course. But here's the twist: these moments are golden opportunities for teaching flexibility, resilience, and the art of improvisation.

First, understanding the impact of missed schedules is crucial. It's more than just a delay; it's a test of patience and adaptability. A study from the field of business psychology suggests that adaptability—how we respond to change—plays a crucial role in determining success. Apply this concept to travel. Each missed schedule is a mini-lesson in adaptability.

Your child learns early that life doesn't always go according to plan, and that's okay.

Strategizing a response is critical. When a flight gets **canceled** or a museum visit is postponed, see it as a puzzle to solve. This is where detailed, specific, actionable planning comes into play. For example, always have a plan B. If you're aiming to visit three attractions in a day and miss one, what's your backup? It's not just making lemonade out of lemons; it's having a lemonade recipe ready just in case.

Finally, execution with grace is where the magic happens. Missing a scheduled event doesn't mean the day is wasted. Transform it into an adventure. Explore a park you hadn't planned on visiting. Find a local eatery off the beaten path. These unplanned experiences can be more memorable than the original schedule. A survey conducted among families who travel frequently revealed that their most cherished memories often came from spontaneous adventures, not the meticulously planned ones.

Think of it like jazz music. The beauty of jazz lies in its improvisation. Traveling with children is similar. You have a basic structure, but the unplanned notes often create the most beautiful melodies. Your family's travel story is unique. It's composed of both planned harmonies and spontaneous riffs.

Remember, missed schedules are not failures; they're

opportunities. Each one teaches your child (and maybe you) something valuable about dealing with life's unpredictability's with a positive attitude.

The Adventure of Staying Healthy

Traveling unfolds a world of wonders for children. It's like opening a book full of stories, each page a new adventure. Yet, amidst the excitement, a tiny invader often overlooked can turn the story sour—**illness**. Keeping healthy on the go is crucial, especially for the little explorers. It's not just about avoiding the cold or flu; it's more about crafting a shield that guards against unseen foes, ensuring the adventure continues uninterrupted.

First off, hydration. It sounds simple, yet it's often forgotten. Children are whirlwinds of energy, quickly losing more fluids than they consume. A dehydrated child can soon go from bouncing with excitement to feeling lethargic. Remember, it's not just water that does the trick.

Rehydration solutions or drinks with electrolytes can be lifesavers, especially in hot climates. In one study, kids engaging in regular outdoor activities reduced their risk of heat-related illnesses by over 50% simply by increasing their fluid intake. The rule of thumb? If they're not asking for water, it's time to offer it.

Then there's food. New cuisines are part of the travel excitement. However, the wrong choices can lead to upset stomachs, taking the fun out of the trip. The solution isn't to avoid local foods but to choose wisely. Opt for freshly cooked meals over raw salads or fruits that can't be peeled. Street food? Go where the locals go; those busy spots speak volumes about food safety. A study showcased how children who were introduced to a variety of foods while young developed a more robust immunity against common foodborne pathogens.

Lastly, never underestimate the power of sleep. It's the ultimate recharge, crucial for daily recovery. Jet lag, changes in schedule, and excitement can disrupt sleep patterns. Stick to routines as much as possible. A well-rested child is a happy explorer. Researchers have found that children who maintain regular sleep schedules while traveling adapt quicker to new environments, showing improved mood and cognitive function.

Each of these tactics, from hydration to sleep, is a piece of the puzzle in staying healthy. Combine them, and you build a fortress, keeping the children safe and ensuring the adventure goes on. Like a knight's armor in battle, these strategies shield them, letting the wonder of travel unfold without interruption. Just as we learned to manage meltdowns and jet lag, tackling health on the road is another chapter in the travel book of life, filled with lessons not just for the trip but for a lifetime.

Travel challenges us, but it also rewards us. It teaches us resilience and adaptability and enriches our lives with memories and experiences. As we explore the world with our children, let's not forget to equip them with the tools and knowledge to stay healthy on the go. Let's give them a love for adventure that lasts a lifetime.

Dr. Robert Walker

Chapter 7
Engaging Activities for Children

Traveling with children is akin to giving them a canvas and a palette of colors, inviting them to paint their masterpieces of experiences. Each destination is a new shade, and each culture is a different brushstroke, creating a rich tapestry of knowledge and memories. **Travel isn't just about seeing new places; it's about opening young minds to the vast world around them.**

Children are naturally curious. The question is, they marvel, and they learn at an astonishing pace. When we travel with them, we're not just taking them on a vacation; we're engaging them in a live classroom where every experience, from trying a new food to hearing a different language, adds to their education.

One study from the Department of Education highlighted that students who participated in cultural exchanges and travel programs showed improved academic performance and a greater understanding of global cultures. These journeys, vivid and teeming with life, offer lessons that no textbook can.

Nurturing Naturalists - The Great Outdoors as a Classroom

Imagine your child as a young explorer, their curiosity as their compass, navigating the forests, mountains, and rivers of our beautiful planet. This is the essence of **Exploring the Great Outdoors**.

Imagine your child as a young explorer, their curiosity as their compass, navigating the forests, mountains, and rivers of our beautiful planet. This is the essence of exploring the great outdoors. It's more than just a chapter theme; it's a fundamental belief that nature itself is an unparalleled classroom, offering lessons in the most interactive, impactful way possible. The fresh air, the myriad species of plants and animals, and the diverse ecosystems are like pages in a living textbook that children can walk through, touch, and experience directly.

For instance, the American Academy of Pediatrics suggests that direct interactions with nature stimulate children's senses in a way that screen-based activities cannot. This sensory play boosts cognitive development and reduces the risk of attention disorders. We're talking about real, tangible benefits here—imagine your child acing their science fair project on local flora and fauna because they've experienced these wonders firsthand!

Practical Steps for Every Family. It's essential to tailor outdoor activities to be both enjoyable and educational. Start simple. A visit to a local national park with a guided nature walk can open up conversations about biodiversity.

Many parks offer junior ranger programs, turning a day trip into an exciting quest filled with tasks and rewards. It's not just about walking and looking; it's about engaging and learning.

Equip your child with a notebook and camera. Encourage them to document different species or interesting natural phenomena they encounter. This small act transforms them from passive observers into active researchers.

Just like the intricate ecosystems they'll explore, children's minds are vibrant and complex. By choosing to expose them to the wonders of the natural world, you're planting the seeds for a lifelong appreciation of our planet. After all, in a world where digital screens often dominate our attention, the simple act of stepping outside with your child can be a radical act of love and learning.

Decoding History and Culture Through Museums

Exploring museums with your children is like unlocking a treasure chest of the world's collective memory. It's here where stories of the past come alive, not just through exhibits but through the immersive experiences they offer. Museums aren't just storage spaces for artifacts; they are gateways to understanding complex cultures and histories in a nuanced way.

The Magic of Museums lies in their power to transform abstract dates and events into tangible experiences. Imagine the spark in your child's eyes as they stand before a dinosaur skeleton, not just learning about the Jurassic period but feeling the awe of time's vastness. Museums offer this unique blend of education and entertainment, making learning about history and culture an engaging, interactive experience.

But here's the kicker - **museums can be more than just visits**; they can be full-on adventures. Many museums offer activities like scavenger hunts, which encourage kids to engage deeply with the exhibits. They're not just looking; they're on a mission. This active participation cements historical and cultural knowledge in a way that passive observation can't.

Making the most of museum visits requires a bit of prep work. Choose museums that match your child's interests—dinosaurs, space, art, or technology. There's a museum for virtually every curiosity. Before your visit, talk about what you'll see; this primes their excitement. During the visit, ask thought-provoking questions: "What do you think life was like when this was used?" or "How does this painting make you feel?" After the visit, encourage them to create something inspired by what they saw. It could be a drawing, a story, or a

DIY project.

It's about more than history. It's about developing critical thinking, understanding perspectives, appreciating diversity, and fostering empathy. These are the underpinnings of global citizenship. Embedded in the act of exploring museums is a powerful lesson—that learning is not confined to classrooms or textbooks. It is all around us, in the stories of those who came before us, in the art they created, and in the technological advances they achieved.

Dr. Robert Walker

The Art of Travel Journaling

Imagine every trip as a blank book, and your child holds the pen. That's the essence of travel journaling. It's a method where experience transforms into a tangible memory. Not only does it serve as a personal keepsake, but it also enhances your child's learning from each adventure.

In the age of digital snapshots and video clips, the act of writing and sketching may seem quaint, yet it's powerfully enriching. Such activities compel children to observe their surroundings more closely. They're not just passing through; they're engaging. This deliberate observation sharpens their attention to detail and boosts their memory recall. Writing about what they've seen, felt, and discovered cements those experiences more deeply in their minds.

Begin with a simple, unlined notebook that allows for both drawing and writing. Next, equip them with a set of pencils, erasers, and maybe some colored pencils or markers. Encourage them to jot down what catches their eye, as well as what they hear, smell, and feel. These notes can be brief; the goal is to capture impressions.

For journaling to become a valuable part of travel, it needs to be consistent. Here's where you can weave in lessons from business psychology about habit formation. Set aside a specific time each day for journaling—maybe during a quiet evening back at the hotel or a midday break at a café. The key is regularity. This structured approach mirrors successful strategies used in habit formation within organizational settings. It's about creating a routine that sticks.

Ask them to research a bit about the places you visit. They can jot down interesting facts or historical data. This blends education with exploration, like gamification of learning, where the reward is the joy of discovery. After the trip, go through the journal together. Discuss their entries. This review session solidifies the learning, akin to a debriefing session in a corporate training scenario. It reinforces the lessons learned and heightens the appreciation of the experience.

Travel journaling is more than just keeping a diary. It's a dynamic way to enhance your child's travel experience. It deepens their learning and enriches their memories, laying a foundation for observing, reflecting, and appreciating the world around them in a mindful manner.

A CHILD INTO THE WORLD

Hands-on Experiences with Local Crafts and Cuisine

Travel isn't just about seeing new places; it's about touching, creating, and tasting the very essence of those destinations. Imagine your child's hands molding clay or weaving textiles under the guidance of a local artisan. These activities do more than create souvenirs; they craft a deeper connection with the place.

When your child actively engages in making a traditional craft, they're not just working with their hands. They're engaging their brains in a way that reading about the experience simply can't match. The smell of the clay, the texture of the fabric, the concentration in their eyes—it's all part of the hands-on learning process.

Now, think about cuisine. Cooking classes offer a window into a culture's soul. Preparing and then sampling a local dish teaches your child about the region's agriculture, history, and preferences. For instance, making a classic Southern dish like gumbo can lead to discussions about the blend of cultures in the American South. Nutritional psychology supports the idea that experiencing new tastes can open children's minds to new ideas and perspectives. It's akin to adding new ingredients to their developmental stew, enriching their growth with every bite.

Every stroke of the brush, kneading of the dough, or stitch in the fabric is a story being told. By participating in these hands-on activities, your child isn't just making something; they're becoming part of a story that's been told for generations. Now, they add their own chapter. It's about more than crafting and cooking; it's about creating global citizens who appreciate the richness of our world's tapestry.

Consider this analogy: just as a chef carefully selects each ingredient to create a harmonious dish, each travel experience you choose for your child adds a unique flavor to their development. These hands-on experiences are the spices that transform a simple dish into a culinary masterpiece, turning a simple trip into a profound learning opportunity.

Incorporate these activities into your travel plans. Look for local workshops and cooking classes. Read reviews and choose those with engaging instructors who are passionate about teaching children. Remember, the goal is engagement, not perfection. It's about the experience, the learning, and the fun.

Traveling with your child is about opening doors to new experiences. Through hands-on experiences with local crafts and cuisine, you're providing them with invaluable lessons in culture, history, and humanity. You're not just exploring the world; you're expanding their minds.

Dr. Robert Walker

Chapter 8
The Art of Slow Travel

The notion of *slow travel* might seem counterintuitive in our fast-paced world. Imagine this - rather than rushing from one landmark to another; you take your time to soak in the beauty of a single street. You're not just a visitor; you're momentarily a local.

Slow travel isn't about how many photos you snap; it's about the stories behind those photos. For instance, spending a day learning to make pasta with a local Italian nonna offers a rich story of connection, far outlasting the memory of queuing for hours at a tourist hotspot. Here, every moment becomes a learning opportunity for your child.

Take a family who decides to spend a month in a small French village. They learn a few phrases in French, shop at the local market, and their children play with the neighborhood kids. They're not just on holiday; they're part of the community. This immersion offers profound lessons in language, culture, and adaptability that a weekend whirlwind trip never could.

By focusing on slow travel, you're also making a contribution to sustainability. It's about putting the brakes on over-tourism and choosing experiences that are kinder to the planet. It's opting for the train ride through the countryside over the plane flight. Every choice becomes a lesson for your child in environmental stewardship.

The Art of Slow Travel is your manual to transforming a family holiday into a rich tapestry of experiences that educates, inspires, and connects. Whether it's learning a craft, understanding local conservation efforts, or simply enjoying the rhythm of daily life in a new place, slow travel redefines what it means to truly see the world.

The Philosophy of Slow Travel

Step into the philosophy of slow travel. Imagine it as a river. Some rivers rush, moving fast, tumbling over rocks, and weaving through narrow channels. Then, there are rivers that meander. These rivers take their time, stretching out in wide, lazy curves, touching more of the landscape. Slow travel is that meandering river; it's about depth, not speed.

When we race from one attraction to the next, we miss the essence of places. Think of visiting the Grand Canyon. You could stand at the rim, snap a photo, and leave. Or, you could hike down into its depths, spending time feeling its vastness and listening to stories from local guides. This is slow travel. You connect. You understand that the Grand Canyon isn't just a spectacular view; it's a story millions of years in the making. Each layer of rock tells a part of that story.

Research backs this up. Studies in business psychology show that immersive experiences improve our cognitive flexibility (8). This means we think better. We solve problems more creatively. For kids, this kind of learning is gold. They learn about geology, yes. But they also learn patience. They learn to see the bigger picture.

Slow travel urges us to live like locals. Consider staying in a small town in Vermont during maple syrup season. You and your family can learn how syrup is made, meet the farmers, and see how the syrup goes from tree to table. You aren't just tourists; you're part of the community, even if just for a little while.

This experience teaches adaptability and appreciation for different ways of life. It's one thing to read about maple syrup production, but it's another to experience it firsthand.

Slow travel is also kinder to our planet. Instead of flying

multiple short distances, you choose one place and explore it deeply. This reduces carbon emissions and combats overtourism. It teaches our children stewardship of the Earth, helping them understand that their travel choices have an impact. Opting for a train ride through the Rockies can be an adventure, but it's also a choice that respects our environment.

In slow travel, every choice we make is a lesson. It's a chance to show our kids what truly matters. We teach them to value experiences over things, to practice patience, and to connect deeply with the world around them.

Mindful Journeys and Eco-conscious Choices

Traveling offers more than just a break from the daily grind. It's a chance to teach our kids about caring for our planet. Think of it like packing a suitcase: every item we choose to bring—or leave behind—matters. Our travel choices are just the same; each decision impacts our world.

First off, consider the footprint of your destination. Some places are working hard to protect their environment. They limit tourists to reduce wear and tear and focus on sustainability. For example, certain national parks in the USA have implemented measures to lower crowd sizes and reduce environmental impact. They encourage visits during off-peak seasons and have switched to cleaner energy sources for their operations. This doesn't just ease the strain on natural resources; it also offers a better, less crowded experience. When planning your trip, look for destinations that value sustainability as much as you do.

Next, think about how you get there. Air travel dumps tons of carbon dioxide into the atmosphere. While it's sometimes necessary, there are often greener options. Trains, for example, emit far less CO_2 per passenger than planes and can offer scenic views and a comfy ride. If you're staying stateside, consider a train trip across the country. You'll see the landscape change in ways you'd miss from 30,000 feet up. If driving is your only option, think about renting a hybrid or electric vehicle. Many car rental companies now offer these options at competitive rates.

Think of it this way: our planet is like a library. Each forest, river, and mountain has stories to tell. When we travel mindfully, we're not just visitors; we're listeners. We teach our children to hear those stories, to respect them, and to make choices that ensure those stories live on for generations to come.

By integrating these eco-conscious choices into our travels, we not only minimize our environmental impact but also enrich our travel experiences. These actions teach our children the importance of sustainability and the role they can play in preserving our planet. The memories we create, the lessons we impart, and the impact we leave behind—every bit counts in the grand tapestry of eco-conscious travel.

Patience as a Travel Companion

Traveling teaches us many things. Above all, patience stands out as a key lesson, especially in slow travel. Picture this: you're on a long train ride across the USA. The landscape shifts outside your window—from towering mountains to expansive deserts, the scene changes gradually. Here, patience isn't just a virtue; it's a necessity.

In today's world, we want everything fast: fast food, fast internet, fast travel. Slow travel goes against this grain. It teaches us to wait, to observe, to experience deeply. This is crucial for our kids. They learn that some things—the best things—take time.

Imagine waiting for a bus in a small American town. The schedule isn't rushed. You and your kids have time to explore, talk to locals, and see things you'd otherwise miss. This scenario teaches your children patience in a real, tangible way. They learn the value of slowing down. They see that waiting can lead to unexpected adventures.

Patience fosters emotional intelligence. It teaches kids to deal with frustration and delays without getting upset. This is a life skill—something they'll use every day, not just when traveling. It reduces stress. It makes us happier.

When travel plans go awry, as they often do, patience becomes critical. It's about solving problems calmly. It's about looking at a delayed flight as an extra chapter in your adventure. This mindset is powerful. It turns challenges into opportunities for learning and growth.

Slow travel and patience are closely linked. Choosing a train ride over a plane isn't just good for the planet; it teaches kids to enjoy the journey itself, not just the destination. This aligns with our eco-conscious travel ethos. We're not just traveling; we're teaching our children to care for our world.

Think of patience like a muscle. The more you use it, the stronger it gets. Each slow travel experience is a workout for your patience muscle. Over time, your family becomes stronger, more adaptable, better prepared to handle whatever comes your way.

Slow travel also immerses us in local cultures, and this requires patience. Learning about local customs and languages takes time. It's not something you can rush. This immersion teaches respect, fosters understanding, and bridges gaps.

In travel and in life, patience opens doors. It teaches us to appreciate each moment. It shows our kids the value of waiting, of experiencing, of truly living. In a world that moves at lightning speed, this lesson is priceless.

Dr. Robert Walker

Chapter 9
Harnessing Technology for Enhanced Travel Experiences

Think about it. Today, a smartphone in our pocket can be more informative than a seasoned tour guide, and a travel app can reveal hidden gems in a city within minutes. It's like having a magic wand that creates memorable experiences with a swipe and a tap.

First things first, technology is not the enemy of authentic travel experiences. Instead, it's an enabler. For instance, GPS has transformed the way we explore new places. Remember the times of bulky maps and confusing directions? Now, with real-time navigation, we venture into unknown territories with confidence, making more time for adventure and less for getting lost.

Travel apps are not just about navigation and safety; they're a goldmine for **educational content**. Interactive guides and AR apps turn boring historical facts into engaging stories for kids. It's like being in a classroom without walls, where history, art, and culture come alive in front of their eyes.

This chapter isn't just about showing you which apps to download. It's about understanding how to leverage technology to enrich your family's travels, making them safer, more educational, and unforgettable. By integrating these digital tools thoughtfully, we can elevate our travel experiences, turning every trip into an opportunity for our children to learn and grow in ways we never imagined possible.

Gone are the days of technology being a mere distraction. Welcome to an era where it's your passport to a world brimming with possibilities.

Innovative Learning Tools on the Go

Thanks to innovative learning tools, traveling with kids has evolved from passive sightseeing to interactive and educational experiences. Imagine turning historical landmarks into a playground of knowledge or the night sky into a personal planetarium. This isn't just possible; it's easy with the right apps and gadgets.

Augmented Reality - Apps like **TimeLooper** reinvent how children learn history. Standing in front of the Liberty Bell, they can view a reenactment of its last ringing through their screens. It's not merely reading about history; it's experiencing it. This method has a powerful impact on retention and comprehension. Studies suggest immersive learning boosts engagement, and kids are more likely to remember what they've "seen" and "done (1)."

Stargazing Apps - Apps such as **Star Walk** transform a night under the stars into a lesson in astronomy. Point your device at the sky, and the app labels the stars, planets, and constellations in real time. It's akin to having an astronomer in your pocket. These apps make learning about the universe accessible anywhere, anytime.

Language Learning - The immersion doesn't end with sights; it extends to languages. **Duolingo** offers bite-sized lessons, making language learning fun and effective. Imagine your child ordering gelato in Italian, thanks to the lessons they took during the flight. It's practical knowledge gained joyfully.

Integrating these tools into your travels does more than educate; it inspires. Children see the world as a classroom without walls. Every experience is a lesson. Every lesson is an adventure. And isn't that the most enthralling way to learn?

These digital tools bridge the gap between education and

entertainment. They embody the modern mantra — learn anytime, anywhere. You're not just giving your child a trip; you're expanding their world, lesson by lesson.

Remember, the key to leveraging these tools effectively lies in choice. Select apps that ignite your child's interest. Make learning a shared adventure. Encourage questions. Seek answers together. This approach nurtures a lifelong love for learning.

In conclusion, innovative learning tools transform travel from mere sightseeing into dynamic, educational experiences. They foster a deeper understanding of the world. More than that, they prepare your child for a future where learning and adaptability are paramount. These tools are not just enhancing travel; they're shaping the global citizens of tomorrow.

Dr. Robert Walker

The Art of Digital Storytelling

Turn Journeys into Narratives. Every trip you take with your family is a story waiting to be told. The art of digital storytelling enables parents and children alike to capture these moments in the most vivid format possible. Think of it as building a time capsule with videos, photographs, and blogs. It's the narrative of your adventures, preserved digitally for years to come.

Why Storytelling Matters. We tell stories to remember. To connect. To grow. Digital storytelling, in particular, teaches invaluable skills. Children learn to narrate their experiences, enhancing their communication capabilities. They learn the basics of photography and video editing, which boosts their technical skills. But most importantly, they learn to see the world through a story's lens, transforming every trip into a learning opportunity.

Getting Started is Simple. You don't need sophisticated gear. A smartphone or a digital camera is sufficient. For blogging, platforms like WordPress or Medium offer user-friendly interfaces for any age. Start by encouraging your kids to take photos of anything that catches their eye. Teach them to question why they find some scenes captivating. Is it the color? The emotion it evokes?

Next, explore videography. Small projects like a day at the beach or a hike through the forest can be great starting points. Video editing apps such as iMovie for Apple users or KineMaster for Android users offer easy-to-learn editing suites.

For blogging, encourage your child to write about their day. It doesn't have to be long. A couple of paragraphs reflecting on their favorite parts of the trip or something new they learned can be very insightful. Over time, they develop a keen eye for detail and a richer understanding of their experiences.

Tell a Story, Build a Memory. Compare digital storytelling to crafting a quilt. Each piece of content—be it a photo, a blog post, or a video—represents a patch in the quilt. Alone, each piece holds value. Together, they create a masterpiece of memories. This quilt not only blankets your family with the warmth of cherished adventures but also becomes a valuable educational tool.

Case Study - The New Journalists. Consider the story of a family who documented their road trip across the 50 states. They used a mix of blogs, vlogs, and social media updates. The children took charge of capturing photos and videos. By the trip's end, they had not just traveled; they had told a story. Their narrative showcased learning in action—from geography lessons at national parks to history lessons at historical sites. Their followers didn't just see photos; they engaged in a learning experience.

In essence, digital storytelling is about more than preserving memories. It's a dynamic way to engage with the world. It transforms passive consumers into active creators. And it does so while teaching critical life skills. Through the act of documenting their travels, children become adept storytellers, proficient photographers, and keen observers of the world around them. They become, in every sense, explorers of both the physical and digital worlds.

Smart Travel - Technology as Your Ultimate Trip Companion

First off, **navigation apps** are not just about finding the quickest route from point A to B. They're about discovering the heartbeat of a new place. Tools like Google Maps go beyond mere directions. They offer real-time traffic updates, public transport schedules, and even bike routes. For families exploring urban landscapes, these apps are critical. They reduce the stress of navigation, making travel smoother.

Then there's the world of **accommodation and restaurant recommendations.** Platforms like Airbnb and Booking.com have revolutionized where we stay. They provide detailed filters that cater to families' unique needs. Want a crib or a kitchenette? No problem. TripAdvisor and Yelp, on the other hand, turn dining into an adventure. They offer insights from real people. You discover hidden gems that no travel guide would tell you about.

Lastly, remember **emergency services apps.** They are the unsung heroes of smart travel. Apps like Red Panic Button or Medical ID allow you to send an SOS with your location. For parents, it's peace of mind in your pocket. You hope never to use it, but it's there, just in case.

To bring this into perspective, think of your family as a team of explorers. You're venturing into the unknown, armed with digital tools that make every aspect of your journey easier, more enjoyable, and safer. It's not just about seeing the world; it's about experiencing it in a way that's thoughtful, engaging, and profoundly enriching.

Smart travel technology doesn't replace the spontaneity and wonder of travel. It enhances it. It ensures that the memories you're creating are about the joy of exploration, not the stress of planning. In this digital age, being a tech-savvy traveler means you're also a smart traveler. And that's a powerful lesson in adaptability and problem-solving for your children. They learn that technology, when used wisely, is not just a convenience; it's a bridge to the world.

As we set our sights beyond the horizon, guided by the digital compass of our era, the essence of travel remains unchanged — it's about discovery, connection, and the stories we weave with each step we take. Technology, in its multifaceted roles, enhances this essence, making every trip not just a departure from the familiar but an entry into a world of new possibilities.

Dr. Robert Walker

Chapter 10
Weaving Memories Into Stories - The Journey Beyond

Here we take a step back. We look at the scattered pieces of our travels - the photos, the souvenirs, the laughter, and even the occasional mishaps. And we start piecing them together into a coherent narrative.

This isn't just about scrapbooking or journaling. It's about understanding how each trip shapes your child and your family. Think of it as editing a movie where each travel experience is a different scene. Your job is to weave these scenes into a story that teaches and inspires.

It helps children process experiences and learn from them. In a way, turning travel memories into stories is an exercise in lifelong learning. You're not just reminiscing. You're teaching your children how to reflect, learn, and grow from their experiences. This goes beyond the basic **"What did we see?"** to deeper questions like **"What did we learn?"** and **"How did this change us?"**

The act of reflecting on your travels is a form of storytelling. But it's also a learning opportunity. Encourage your children to think about the places they've visited. What stood out for them? How did it feel to stand in the shadow of a monument they'd only seen in books? Reflection turns experiences into lessons. And it's those lessons that stick with us.

Innovative Memory Preservation Techniques

Crafting Memory Boxes - Think of a memory box as a treasure chest for your family's adventures. It's simple yet profoundly impactful. Start with any box that resonates with your family's style. Each trip can have its own box, or you can create a yearly box for all travels. What goes inside? Everything that sparks joy and brings back memories.

Ticket stubs, maps, postcards, and even a small vial of sand from a beach visit. The key is to involve your children in choosing what makes the cut. This activity not only declutters your home of souvenirs but also declutters your mind, leaving only the most cherished memories highlighted. It's a tangible form of Marie Kondo's philosophy but for your travel memories.

Creating Art from Souvenirs - Now, this is where fun meets creativity. Transform souvenirs into art. A simple example is creating a collage from brochures and tickets or turning sea shells into a decorative piece. Why not frame a particularly beautiful map you used on a road trip? These art pieces become conversation starters in your home, a silent storyteller of your family's adventures. It's a visual reminder of the joy you shared. Plus, it's a fantastic way to spend a rainy day indoors, getting crafty with your kids.

Digital Storytelling Platforms - In the digital age, storytelling has taken on new dimensions. Websites and apps allow you to create digital scrapbooks or blogs where you can upload photos, videos, and text. Here's the twist. Don't just make it a chronological catalog of your trip. Instead, frame it as a story. Start with a challenge your family faced during the trip and how you overcame it. Maybe it was navigating the subway in a foreign city. This builds narrative tension and keeps readers engaged. Each post can end with a "lesson learned" or "fun fact," making it educational, not just for your children but for everyone who reads it.

Global Citizenship Through Reflection

In today's interconnected world, fostering a mindset of global citizenship in our children is not just important; it's imperative. **Global citizenship** is about understanding the complexities of our world, recognizing our place within it, and acting with empathy and responsibility. It's not about having a passport filled with stamps but about the lessons learned and the perspectives gained from those travels.

Think of it this way - Traveling is like opening a book that offers a plethora of real-life stories, waiting to instill wisdom, empathy, and knowledge. Each trip with your child provides fresh content for this book, with chapters that can mold them into informed, compassionate, and global citizens. Our role as parents is to ensure these stories don't just passively sit there but actively shape our children's worldview.

Reflecting on cultural understanding is a powerful aspect of this. When children are introduced to different cultures, they don't just see the differences; they begin to understand and appreciate them. For example, dining etiquette can vary significantly from one country to another. In Japan, it is considered polite to slurp your noodles, indicating you are enjoying your meal. In contrast, in the United States, slurping is generally frowned upon. Sharing these tidbits with your children in a fun, engaging way can make them more adaptable and respectful individuals.

Empathy grows exponentially when children are exposed to various living conditions and see firsthand how others live. A visit to a developing country can be an eye-opener for them. It's one thing to tell your child that some people lack access to clean water; it's another for them to see a well as the community's primary water source. Such experiences teach gratitude and humility, profoundly shaping their character.

The interconnectedness of our world becomes evident as children notice the similarities amid the differences. They realize that smiles are universal, that laughter needs no translation, and that kindness is a currency accepted everywhere. This understanding is crucial in today's global economy, where teamwork and cooperation often span continents.

Our Children Will Thank Us

Imagine investing in a stock. It promises not just financial returns but also enriches your life with wisdom, empathy, and global awareness. That's travel for your children. It's an unparalleled investment in their future. Studies show that experiences, not possessions, are the key to long-term happiness (7).

Traveling with kids teaches them adaptability like nothing else can. They learn it's okay not to have all the comforts of home 24/7 and discover the joy of trying new things. This isn't just talk; psychologists endorse the role of new experiences in fostering flexibility and resilience in children.

Consider the numbers. A survey found that 74% of Americans prioritize experiences over products. But it's not just about fun. Kids who travel are more likely to be successful in school and later careers. They're the ones who stand out and have stories that captivate.

It's one thing to read about the Great Plains in a textbook. It's entirely another to stand in the vastness of those fields, feeling the wind and smelling the earth. This firsthand experience embeds knowledge in a way that reading alone cannot.

Travel exposes children to diverse cultures and ideas. It challenges their preconceptions and expands their understanding of the world. Real-life examples? A child might only grasp the concept of poverty from books. Seeing it and empathizing with those living it alters their perspective deeply.

These encounters turn into life lessons. They cultivate gratitude and empathy and become discussions at the dinner table, shaping a child's worldview. Instead of merely knowing, they're understanding. And understanding breeds compassion and action.

Think of travel as the legacy you leave your children, not in the form of physical assets but in memories, experiences, and lessons that mold them into conscientious global citizens. This legacy is priceless.

Your children might not remember every toy they played with, but they will recall the adventure of a family trip. These memories are the glue that bonds and the stories retold at family gatherings, becoming richer with each telling.

This legacy teaches more than just facts. It instills values of curiosity, resilience, and open-mindedness—values that shape leaders, innovators, and empathetic humans. In the end, isn't that what we all wish for our children?

To tie it all together, think about the process of turning cocoa beans into chocolate. It's complex, but the result is sweet and universally loved. Travel, similarly, involves challenges. Yet, it yields experiences that enrich your child's life in ways nothing else can. It's the sweetness of seeing, feeling, and understanding the world that remains with them forever.

A CHILD INTO THE WORLD

The Path Forward

Traveling with your children is not just about the destinations; it's about **the stories you create together**. It's the fabric of memories that clothe the future of your kids with resilience, curiosity, and empathy. Think of each trip as a chapter in the grand book of their early life. What we aim for is not just to fill their lives with experiences but to weave these experiences into the core of their being.

When it comes to traveling as a path forward, the focus shifts to **using past adventures as a foundation** for future exploration. This means not just reminiscing about the fun times but also extracting lessons and insights from each trip. For instance, overcoming a missed flight teaches adaptability and problem-solving. Navigating a new city where English is not the primary language cultivates communication skills and boosts confidence.

To make this actionable, consider maintaining a travel journal with your child. This isn't just any journal. It's a treasure trove filled with **"aha" moments**, challenges overcome, and skills acquired. It could be as simple as learning to pack efficiently or as significant as understanding the value of money in different economies.

Drawing from the **science of experiential learning** and the **theories of emotional intelligence**, we know that hands-on experiences are far more impactful on children's development than theoretical knowledge. Daniel Goleman, a pioneer in EI, suggests that competencies like self-awareness, empathy, and handling emotions are best learned in real settings. Travel provides such settings aplenty.

Consider a study from the Global Education and Skills Forum, which highlighted that students who travel or are exposed to different cultures show a marked improvement in their academic performance and social skills. This isn't just about improved grades. It's about nurturing a generation that's comfortable with differences and sees opportunities where others see barriers.

Now, pivot your perspective. Instead of planning a vacation, think of designing a learning expedition. Before you set off, set goals. What new skills could your trip help develop? Is it navigation, budgeting, or perhaps a new language? Each trip becomes a project with objectives, challenges to overcome, and skills to master.

In essence, *traveling is akin to preparing your child for the world's grand stage.* Each trip rehearses real-life challenges and triumphs. They learn the art of adaptation, the elegance of empathy, and the power of perseverance. It's a rehearsal for life's various acts, performed on the world stage with an ensemble cast of diverse characters, cultures, and challenges.

You're equipping them with the tools they need to thrive in an increasingly globalized world. **The path forward** is paved with these adventures, each one building on the last, preparing your child for the grandest adventure of all - life itself.

I have added three bonus chapters ahead that address other aspects of our children's learning apart from travel. Make sure to check them out!

Dr. Robert Walker

Bonus Chapters

Chapter 11
Guide Right - Preparing a Child for Life

Navigating life's financial waters is no small task. It's akin to setting out on an expedition without a map unless you've had the proper guidance. This is vital for our children. We teach them to swim, ride a bike, and interact with others, but do we focus enough on instilling financial wisdom? It's a foundational skill that's as critical as learning to read or write.

Growing up, I was fortunate to have both my mother and father impart valuable lessons. However, it was my stepfather, Dr. David Robinson, who provided a unique perspective that shaped my understanding of finances in profound ways. While my biological parents emphasized the importance of saving, David introduced me to the practical aspects of managing finances with discipline and foresight. Through his guidance, I learned the importance of living within my means, prioritizing needs over wants, and planning for the future. His pragmatic approach instilled in me a sense of fiscal responsibility, which, along with other lessons learned, continues to guide my financial decisions to this day, complementing the foundational lessons instilled by my mother and father.

Financial Responsibility

Tackle financial basics early. Imagine launching a kite. At first, it wobbles. With the right techniques, it soars. This is like teaching kids about money. Start with basics - saving, spending wisely, and sharing. It sets them up for a steady financial flight.

1. **Saving** - It's the foundation. Every dollar saved is like

a brick in their future fortress. Initiate a savings jar or a bank account. Make it a ritual. Every time they get money, a portion goes into savings. If they save $5 a week in a year, that's $260. That can be substantial for a child.

2. **Wise Spending** - Teach them to think twice before buying. Use real examples. For instance, choosing between a toy that will break easily and a book that lasts longer encourages them to value longevity over instant gratification. This approach cultivates discerning consumers.

3. **Sharing** - Encourage generosity. It could be donating to a charity or buying a gift for a friend. This teaches them money isn't just for personal use. It's a tool for kindness and change.

Bank Accounts

Think of a checking account as a child's first boat in the vast ocean of finance. It's where they can row gently, getting a feel of managing money on a day-to-day basis. A savings account, on the other hand, is like storing treasure on an island, watching it grow over time with interest.

Checking Accounts - Ideal for everyday transactions. It teaches kids the value of tracking spending. Start with a simple account. No need for a fancy ship with all the bells and whistles. Look for ones with no fees. This is key. Fees can eat into their funds. Show them monthly statements. This is their map. It shows where their money sailed off to.

Savings Accounts - Here's where their gold coins accumulate. Interest is the magic of their money growing without lifting a finger. Choose an account with a good interest rate. Every bank has its own treasure map. Some have better rates. Others have fees. Avoid the fees. Aim for high interest. This teaches patience and long-term planning. It's not about the gold gathered in a day but over many moons.

A budget is like a compass for this financial adventure. It guides spending and saving. Compare it to planning a trip: you need to know your destination, the route, and what supplies you'll need. A budget helps with this. It shows kids how to allocate their gold—some for food, some for fun, and some to bury for later.

Start with a simple plan. If they have $100, decide how much goes into savings—maybe 20%, which is $20. Then, what about spending? Set a limit, perhaps $30 for fun things. The rest can be for essentials like gifts or contributions to family expenses. This teaches them to balance desires with needs.

Tools and apps designed for kids can make this more engaging. They often have visuals that help kids see where their money is going. This is their financial GPS and makes the concept of budgeting more tangible.

Understanding the flow of money is crucial. These early lessons in checking and savings accounts set children on a course for financial success. It's not just about the numbers; it's about making wise choices.

Consider this: a survey showed that young adults who had savings accounts as children are more likely to be financially stable in their 20s. It's a concrete step toward a future where they are captains of their own ships, not passengers at the mercy of economic tides.

Investing

Investing might seem like a topic reserved for adults, but it's an essential part of preparing your child for life. Just like opening a savings account teaches them the value of storing away money for the future, understanding investing can show them how money can grow over time. Think of it this way: if savings teach them to be cautious swimmers, investing shows them how to ride the waves.

Begin with simple concepts. Explain that investing is like planting a small seed, which, over time, can grow into a towering tree. For instance, buying a few shares in a company they like, such as a favorite video game manufacturer, can be an exciting way to introduce them to the stock market. Highlight the importance of patience. Show them how $100 invested in a solid company can grow significantly over many years, thanks to the magic of compounding interest.

Use vivid, real-life examples to make abstract concepts more tangible. If they invest $50 in a company, and the stock grows 10% each year for 7 years, it won't just be $50 anymore. It could turn into almost double if they reinvest the earnings. This teaches them long-term vision and the power of patience.

A CHILD INTO THE WORLD

Understanding Taxes

Taxes are like the dues we pay for being members of society. They help fund public services such as schools, roads, and firefighters. Start by explaining that whenever someone earns money, a portion goes back to the community through taxes.

For example, if your child earns $100 from a summer job, they might actually receive $85 after taxes. This is because the government takes a percentage (in this case, 15%) of their earnings.

Filing a tax return is like sending in a report card to the government. It's a summary of how much you earned and how much tax you paid. If you paid too much, you get a refund. If you paid too little, you owe more.

Guide them through a basic tax form, such as the 1040EZ, which is a great starting point for teenagers with simple financial situations. Use real numbers to make it more relatable.

Understanding taxes extends beyond just filling out forms. It's about recognizing the value of community contributions and seeing how individual efforts support the collective good. Every road driven on, every park played in, and every library book checked out is possible because of taxes.

Highlight the importance of accuracy and honesty in reporting income. Mistakes can lead to penalties or audits. Just as investing showed them how money grows over time, understanding taxes teaches them the responsibility that comes with earning. It's all part of the grander life lesson in financial literacy, setting them up for success on their personal journeys toward financial independence.

Golden Nuggets

1. The Decree of Depreciation - Understanding Assets and Liabilities

First off, it's crucial to explain the concept of depreciation, especially when it comes to assets and liabilities. For instance, many see purchasing a car as a rite of passage. However, most cars depreciate over time, losing value the moment they leave the lot.

Teach your child to evaluate whether a big purchase will grow in value or become a financial drain. Real-life example? A new car can lose over 20% of its value within the first year. Contrast this with investing in stocks or a savings account where their money has the potential to grow, emphasizing smarter fiscal choices.

2. The Value of Hard Work - Summer Jobs and Financial Independence

Summer jobs are more than a way to prevent boredom; they are a foundational step toward financial independence. By earning their own money, children learn the value of hard work and the sweet victory of purchasing something with money they've earned.

For example, if your child saves $500 from a summer job, they can decide how much to save, spend, or invest. This real-life budgeting exercise teaches them financial planning and the importance of saving for larger goals.

3. The Power of 'No' - Setting Financial Boundaries

Learning to say 'no' to unnecessary spending and peer pressure is a golden nugget of wisdom that will serve your child well into adulthood. This teaches them about setting financial boundaries and the importance of being selective with their spending.

Consider the scenario where their friend is buying the latest smartphone every year. Empower your child to assess their actual needs versus wants, potentially saving them hundreds of dollars and instilling the value of contentment over consumerism.

Book Recommendation - "The Millionaire Next Door"

If there's one book to introduce your child to the world of finance and wealth-building, it's "The Millionaire Next Door" by Thomas J. Stanley and William D. Danko. This eye-opening read uses research and interviews with millionaires to uncover the common characteristics and habits that lead to financial success.

The Millionaire Next Door provides actionable insights into how truly wealthy people avoid extravagant spending in favor of building long-term wealth. It's a powerful lesson for children - being flashy doesn't equate to being rich.

For example, the book highlights that millionaires often drive older vehicles and live in modest homes well below their means. This behavior allows them to invest and accumulate wealth over time, a strategy known as wealth compounding. Here's a number to ponder—over 80% of millionaires are self-made, emphasizing the impact of wise investment and spending choices.

The book is a treasure trove of lessons on assessing value over price. Teaching children to discern between what something costs and what value it brings to their lives is crucial. This differentiation challenges the instant gratification trend pervasive in today's society. Imagine teaching your child to ask, "Will this purchase bring long-term satisfaction, or is it a fleeting desire?" This mindset shift encourages smarter spending and saving habits conducive to building wealth.

One of the book's core tenets is living below one's means. It isn't about depriving oneself but being strategic with spending to ensure financial security and growth. Instill in your child the concept of budgeting—not as a restriction but as a tool for financial freedom. Use a clear example: if you save and invest $100 a month from age 25, assuming an average return of 7%, you'll have over $200,000 by age 65. This illustration emphasizes the power of saving early and the impact of compound interest.

In essence, introducing your child to the principles outlined in *The Millionaire Next Door* can be likened to giving them a financial roadmap for success. By teaching them the value of hard work, responsible spending, and investing early on, you're setting them up for a lifetime of financial independence and security. It's a gift that keeps on giving—empowering your child with the knowledge and tools needed to make sound financial decisions and build wealth for their future.

Chapter 12
Connection with God for Life

Starting this chapter, I want you to recall the sense of direction we give our kids in matters of finance from the last section. Just as we guide them through the complexities of financial responsibility, establishing a connection with God lays another foundational stone in their life's journey. It's about anchoring their souls to something larger than life itself.

Introducing your child to spirituality through practices like attending church, praying before bed, and saying grace can be as enriching as the world travels for which we advocate. These moments are bridges connecting them to gratitude, community, and a deeper sense of purpose. Just as travel opens their eyes to new cultures and perspectives, a connection with God opens their heart to empathy, kindness, and understanding.

Why is this important? Studies in developmental psychology suggest that children with a spiritual or religious foundation tend to show higher resilience against life's adversities. Think about it this way: building a spiritual connection for them is like installing an internal compass. It guides them when the roadmap is unclear, offering comfort and direction amidst life's storms.

The Role of the Church

In the fabric of American society, the church isn't just a building; it's a community hub. **It's where values**

intertwine with life's big questions. Just as we've unpacked the importance of financial literacy and independence in raising well-rounded children, the concept of church merits attention. Here, we pivot from financial charts and compound interest to exploring spiritual dividends.

Church services are more than Sunday rituals. They foster a space where children learn about empathy, community responsibility, and the art of giving back. It's akin to a workshop on humanity. Think of it as enriching their soul's resume. Surveys reveal that children engaged in church activities are more likely to volunteer and help others. This isn't coincidental; it's the training ground for compassion.

As a child, my parents made it a priority to take us to church—Brown Chapel CME Church in Camilla—instilling in us the importance of spirituality from a young age. Sunday mornings were filled with anticipation as we eagerly joined our family in worship, surrounded by the warmth of our church community. Through hymns, prayers, and sermons, we were enveloped in a sense of belonging and purpose, experiencing the profound impact of faith firsthand.

Beyond the walls of the church, the values and teachings imparted during those formative years became guiding lights in our lives. Spirituality provided us with a moral compass, instilling virtues of compassion, integrity, and resilience. It taught us to seek solace in times of adversity and to celebrate blessings with gratitude. The foundation of faith laid in childhood continues to shape our character and decisions, serving as a source of strength and comfort throughout life's journey.

Workshops and community service projects linked with churches provide hands-on experience. **Children see firsthand the impact of their efforts.** Whether it's a food drive or a clean-up day, the lesson is clear. Their actions matter. Real-life impact trumps theoretical knowledge every time. Here's a compelling number - 78% of youths involved in church-led community service express a heightened sense of purpose.

Why should parents care? Engaging your child in church isn't just about spirituality. It's about instilling a sense of bigger belonging and purpose. Remember, we're not merely raising kids to survive the world but to change it for the better. In essence, church attendance and involvement seed the next generation of community leaders, empathetic allies, and proactive citizens.

Dr. Robert Walker

Pray Before You Go to Bed

After discussing the role of the church in fostering community and individual growth, we pivot to the power of **personal prayer**--specifically, the practice of praying before bed. This nightly ritual can be a crucial spiritual touchstone for children, akin to a psychological unwinding, offering both comfort and connectivity.

Why pray at night? Consider this like hitting the pause button on a day filled with activity, challenges, and learning. For children, the act of praying before bed helps process the day's events. It's a moment of quiet reflection in their otherwise bustling lives. A nightly prayer does just that. It's their own private moment to express gratitude, seek guidance, or simply find solace.

The benefits? They're tangible. Studies show children who

engage in regular prayer or meditative practices demonstrate improved attention spans and reduced anxiety (9). They learn early on the value of introspection and the strength found in seeking inner peace. In practice, it's quite simple; however, the outcomes are profound. Guidance through prayer teaches resilience. When faced with a challenge, instead of panicking, a child might recall the comforting routine of prayer, tapping into a well of calm.

Consider a child facing a tough math test. Instead of fretting, they reflect during their nightly prayer, asking for focus and clarity. The next day, they approach the test with a steadier hand. This isn't magic; it's the psychological benefit of developing a resilient, reflective mindset. Building this habit also underlines the importance of ending each day with a positive, reflective note, ensuring children understand the significance of processing experiences, both good and bad.

Start simple. Encourage your child to spend a few moments each night reflecting on their day and expressing whatever thoughts come to their mind. It can begin as a sharing session with you, eventually evolving into a personal practice. The key here is making it a consistent routine, not a chore. And remember, the goal is to instill a sense of peace and reflection, creating a spiritual bookmark at the end of each day.

Say Grace Before You Eat

Transitioning from the spiritual calm of nightly prayers, we steer into another practice deeply rooted in both tradition and value--saying grace before meals. This simple act holds more than meets the eye, especially for children. It's not merely about giving thanks for the food on the table but about cultivating an attitude of gratitude and mindfulness in life.

Gratitude Grows. For children, saying grace can be their first step into a world where gratitude is a daily practice. It's a lesson in looking beyond oneself and appreciating the abundance of what they have. It teaches them to pause, reflect, and acknowledge.

A Mindful Moment. Saying grace is also an exercise in mindfulness. It's a break in the day, a moment to stop and really consider the present. For kids, these few seconds can be a beacon of calm in their otherwise chaotic days. It shows them the importance of slowing down. Like a mindfulness bell, it brings attention back to the now, to the communal and personal joy of sharing a meal.

Start this practice with enthusiasm. Share its importance in simple terms. Make it a joyful moment, not a chore. It could be as straightforward as, "We say thank you for this food and the hands that made it." Involve them. Ask what they're thankful for each day. You might be surprised by their insights.

Saying grace knits the fabric of family together, strengthening bonds over shared expressions of thankfulness. It encapsulates the essence of what we've navigated through in previous chapters—the power of routine, the value of reflection, and the teaching of resilience.

In a world where meals are often hurried and attention is fragmented, this practice calls us back to a communal spirit. Like the gears of a clock synchronized to mark each moment with precision, saying grace ensures that the family unit moves in harmony, aware and appreciative of the present.

Through this, children learn to view their meals, and indeed their lives, through a lens of gratefulness. It's a simple yet profound ripple that can turn into a wave of positive change in their demeanor and interactions. Remember, in instilling the practice of saying grace, you're not just teaching manners; you're sowing the seeds for a lifetime of gratitude and mindfulness.

Thank God for His Blessing

Connecting with God moves beyond the rituals; it's the acknowledgment of blessings that often go unnoticed. It's like the Wi-Fi of spirituality—silent yet omnipresent. You don't see it, but you know it's there because your life is functioning smoother with it. When children learn to thank God for His blessings, they start seeing the world not just as a place where demands are made but as a space filled with gifts waiting to be acknowledged. This mindset transformation is crucial. It's not about religion. It's about gratitude.

Gratitude Alters Perception. Imagine your child thanking God every night, not for the grand gestures but for the small, almost invisible blessings—like a friend's smile or a sunny day. Psychologists have found that gratitude increases life satisfaction and decreases stress levels. It's akin to mental alchemy, turning ordinary metal into gold in the mind's eye.

Start by modeling gratitude. Thank your child for small acts of kindness. Make it a dinner table activity where each family member thanks God for one unnoticed blessing of the day. Encourage your child to keep a gratitude journal. The act of writing magnifies the feeling of gratitude, reinforcing its benefits.

This ties directly into the journeys we take—both physical and spiritual. While travel expands our horizons outward, gratitude expands them inward. It teaches children to be attentive, to see the world with wonder, to appreciate their place in it, and, most importantly, to acknowledge the blessings that pave their paths, sunlit or shadowed.

In this era of fast-paced living, taking a moment to whisper a "thank you" for the seemingly mundane—like the buzzing bees or the freedom to express—can ground children in a reality where every bit counts. It's a lesson in humility. It's an exercise in awareness.

In sum, teaching children to thank God for His blessings is not an abstract concept. It's a concrete tool. It equips them with a lens to see the world not as a series of challenges but as a mosaic of blessings. This perspective is priceless. It can't be bought, but it can be taught. And it starts with us, the parents, leading by example.

Chapter 13
Participation in Sports or Other Activities

Picture this - just like navigating the twists and turns of a new city can enrich your child's perspective, engaging in sports or various activities equips them with skills for life's game. It's more than just play.

First up, **team sports.** They are not just about winning or losing. Children learn about teamwork. They understand the value of working with others to achieve a common goal. **Solo sports**, on the other hand, teach self-reliance and discipline. Each type of sport offers its unique lesson, akin to the diverse cultures encountered during travel.

Consider this stat from *Youth Sports Statistics* - over 75% of children participate in organized sports every year. The lessons they learn? Invaluable. They gain resilience and learn about dedication and the importance of hard work.

But it's not all about sports. Chess, drama, and robotics clubs offer cerebral and creative challenges. They craft thinkers and innovators. Each activity is a brick in the foundation of their future.

Life is the biggest adventure your child will undertake. Just as travel opens their eyes, sports and activities shape their character. They teach resilience, teamwork, and dedication. These lessons are the tools they'll carry into adulthood. Equip them well.

Get Involved at an Early Age

The Foundation of Success Lies in Early Engagement. Just like providing your child with a varied diet supports their physical growth, early involvement in sports and activities nurtures their emotional and social development. It's simple. The skills children learn on the field, in the gym, or at club meetings become the scaffold upon which their future selves are built. This is not about grooming pro athletes or chess masters. It's about setting a pattern of active, engaged living.

Start young. The benefits are too big to ignore. Research shows that children who engage in activities from an early age develop better communication skills. They also show higher levels of empathy. Why? Because these settings teach them to understand and respond to different perspectives. It's a mini-model of the real world. They learn to celebrate victories with grace and accept losses with dignity. *Imagine it as training wheels for life.* Whenever they fall, they learn to get back up.

But it's not just soft skills. **Numbers speak loud.** A study from the University of Michigan highlights that young children involved in extracurricular activities are 85% more likely to stay in school. This isn't about keeping them busy; it's about instilling a sense of belonging and commitment. These children build a diverse skill set. They juggle schedules. They learn time management early on. It's akin to planting a tree. The right care and environment will see it grow strong and sturdy.

The transition to adolescence and young adulthood is smoother. Teens engaged in activities are less likely to succumb to peer pressure. They're busy, after all. They have little time for trouble. Plus, they have a community—a sense of identity. This buffers against many of the mental health challenges youths face today.

In essence, encouraging participation in sports and activities is a preemptive strike against a host of future challenges. It offers children a playbook for life. And as parents, isn't that the ultimate goal? We need to prepare our children for the game of life, equipped not just to play but to win.

Link to Previous Learning. Much like our chapter on the financial wisdom of planning and saving for travel, engaging your child in activities from an early age is about investment. It's about investing time, energy, and sometimes money into their holistic development. The return? A well-rounded, capable, and resilient adult.

Remember, your role is pivotal. Your support and encouragement are the wind beneath their wings. Be present. Cheer them on. Celebrate their efforts. Correct with kindness. Your engagement in this process is as crucial as theirs. After all, every champion once had a cheerleader who believed in them before they believed in themselves.

Empowering Choices - Letting Your Child Lead

Understanding autonomy in development is key. Think of it as letting your child drive while you're in the passenger seat with a map. They choose the route. You offer guidance when needed. This approach doesn't just apply to navigating the roads during a family trip; it's crucial in deciding their interests and commitments, especially in sports and other activities.

It's about value, not volume. Don't just fill their schedule. Fill their need for exploration and self-discovery. A study published in the *American Journal of Family Psychology* highlights that children who choose their extracurricular activities are more engaged and show improved time management and organizational skills. The numbers are telling. These kids are 70% more likely to continue their chosen activity into adolescence.

The role of choice is paramount. We've seen it in the business world. Employees who have a say in their projects are 65% more productive. The same principle applies here. When children decide whether to stick with a sport or activity, they're not just choosing how to spend their afternoon. They're learning decision-making. They're weighing the pros and cons. They're prioritizing. It's a mini-executive training program, and the skills they develop are transferable to every area of their lives.

Consider this an investment. Yes, there might be a financial outlay for soccer cleats or chess club memberships. But what you're really investing in is your child's growth and satisfaction. Satisfaction that comes from making their own decisions. The return on investment is a confident, autonomous, and resilient young person.

But remember the safety net. Your role isn't obsolete. It's just shifted. Be there to catch them if they fall. Offer advice when asked. Praise their effort, not just their achievements. Your involvement is their safety net.

In sum, letting your child lead in the choice of their activities is not about taking a backseat. It's about co-piloting their developmental journey. It teaches them not just to play a sport or perform a skill but to make choices that align with their interests and values. This, in essence, prepares them not just for the game of life but for winning at it.

A CHILD INTO THE WORLD

Show Your Support

When it comes to your child's involvement in sports or other activities, think of yourself as their ultimate fan club president. **Your support means more than you might realize.** It's like the fuel in their tank, propelling them forward.

Be present. This doesn't just mean showing up to games or performances, though that's crucial. It means being mentally and emotionally present, too. Listen to them talk about their day, their challenges, their successes. Offer encouragement over criticism. A pat on the back or a "Great job!" can work wonders for their confidence. Remember, it's about building them up, not just their skills.

Encourage, but don't pressure. There's a fine line between supporting and pushing. Your role? Help them find their own balance. Guide them in setting realistic goals. Celebrate the effort, not just the outcome. This approach helps frame challenges as opportunities for growth. It's a mindset that, once developed, seeps into every facet of their life. They learn resilience. They understand that falling isn't failing; it's a chance to rise even stronger.

Treat setbacks as learning opportunities. Every athlete or performer faces setbacks. Michael Jordan didn't make his high school basketball team on his first try. Yet, he's known as one of the greatest basketball players of all time. Why? Because he saw that setback as a challenge to overcome, not a verdict on his ability. Share stories like these with your child. It shows them that every great success story has chapters of struggle. It's all part of the game.

In short, your support can turn the tide for your child's experience in sports and activities. It's like being the roots that allow a tree to weather any storm. Strong, unyielding, and forever nourishing. Show up, cheer loudly, and watch them soar.

Chapter 14
There Will Be Mistakes

In our journey through life, just as in traveling, we're bound to take a wrong turn or two. It's inevitable. Mistakes are the pit stops, not the end of the road. Think of them as the tourist traps on the map of parenting. You know they're there, and you try to avoid them, but somehow, you end up taking that exit anyway. And that's okay.

Mistakes are not failures but lessons in disguise. Each one teaches us something new about ourselves and how we relate to our children. It's through these experiences that we learn resilience, adaptability, and patience. Not just us, but our kids, too. They see us stumble, get up, dust ourselves off, and keep going. This is an invaluable lesson.

Imagine you're learning to ride a bike. You wouldn't expect to pedal perfectly on the first try. There will be wobbles. Maybe even a fall. Parenting is similar. You start off unsure, maybe a bit wobbly. Sometimes, you might even fall. But the key lies in getting back up, learning from what sent you sideways, and trying again.

Here's a chunk of wisdom to munch on: according to research, children who observe their parents overcoming obstacles are more likely to develop persistence (10). This doesn't mean we intentionally make mistakes in front of our kids. But it does mean we don't hide them. We own up. We show them how we learn and adapt.

For instance, a study published in *Developmental Psychology* found that children whose parents openly discuss their mistakes and what they learned from them tend to develop a 'growth mindset.' This mindset encourages the belief that abilities can be developed through dedication and hard work.

But how do we put this into practice? Start by sharing. When you make a mistake, talk about it at the dinner table. Explain what happened, what you learned, and what you'll do differently next time. Make it a story—your very own family fable. Stories stick. They teach.

Remember, the goal isn't to be a perfect parent. There's no

such thing. The aim is to be a real one. One who messes up, owns it, and grows from it. This is the essence of what travel teaches us—adaptability, resilience, and the joy of discovery, not just of places but of ourselves.

In conclusion, the path of parenting is much like navigating an unfamiliar city. You will make wrong turns. You'll encounter dead ends. But it is these experiences that enrich your journey, teaching invaluable lessons not just to you but to your children and watching how you navigate the map of life. **Mistakes are the landmarks of learning**, and every wrong turn is a step toward growing together.

I want to leave you with a song by John Legend,
'I Know Better' beautifully encapsulates this idea.

They say to Sing what you know.
But I've sung what they want.
Some folks do what they're told.
But baby, this time, I won't
Will look through that door
I know the truth won't lie
Some things I've done before I can't justify
There are kings in my past
Things no one can be proud of
But I stand in the light I've cast
And turn away from any lack of love

Dr. Robert Walker

Oh, and I walked through that door
I say here I go
You see me and nothing more
I'm singing what I know
I know better
I know better
Legend is just a name
I know better than to be so proud
I won't drink in all this fame
I'll take more love than I'm allowed
I won't have to cut it off from where it came
My history has brought me to this place
This power and the color of my face
And I know better, oh, oh

I know better
Oh! I'll rise from the floor if I don't win
I'll bust open that door, so let me in
And the music chooses me to sing. I let her
I'll sing what I know, yes
I know better, oh
I know better, yes
I know better
I know better

I Know Better - John Legend

Epilogue

As I reach the final pages of this book, my mind wanders back to the journey that inspired these words—the travels I've shared with my family, the adventures still waiting on the horizon, and the discovery that has fueled my passion for opening young minds to our wondrous world.

While the destinations have come and gone, flitting by like colorful leaves dancing on the wind, the lessons of each trip remain etched deeply in my soul. It is those lessons that I hope to pass on to you, the reader, and to parents and families alike—that travel is so much more than a fleeting good time or a collection of photos in an album. It is an investment in our future, a toolkit for building resilient, compassionate children ready to take on life's adventures.

As I close this chapter of my story, I do so with optimism for the book's power to foster curious minds and open new gateways of discovery. May each turned page spark wonder, each destination stirs the imagination, and each journey forge memories to last a lifetime. Our world awaits the eager eyes of our youth, and I can think of no better teachers than experience, empathy, and the endless magic of watching children see the vast tapestry of life unfurling before them with each new horizon crossed.

The adventures, my friends, have only just begun.

References

1. Boston University Center for Teaching & Learning. Experiential learning [Internet]. 2017 [cited 2024 Apr 24]. Available from: https://www.bu.edu/ctl/ctl_resource/experiential-learning/
2. Doraiswamy PM, London E, Varnum P, Harvey B, Saxena S, Tottman S, et al. Empowering 8 Billion Minds: Enabling Better Mental Health for All via the Ethical Adoption of Technologies. NAM Perspectives [Internet]. 2019 Oct 28;2019. Available from: http://dx.doi.org/10.31478/201910b
3. Medina J. Brain Rules for Baby, Updated and Expanded: How to Raise a Smart and Happy Child from Zero to Five. Pear Press; 2014. 336 p.
4. Park SY, Pan B, Ahn JB. Family Trips and Academic Achievement in Early Childhood. Annals Of Tourism Research [Internet]. 2020 Jan 1 [cited 2024 Apr 25];80(2). Available from: https://www.researchgate.net/publication/337032559_Family_Trips_and_Academic_Achievement_in_Early_Childhood
5. New York State Education Department. WestEd. 2017 [cited 2024 Apr 24]. Zone of Proximal Development: An affirmative perspective in teaching ELLs. Available from: https://www.wested.org/resources/zone-of-proximal-

development/

6. Wang Z, Zhang D, Zheng Z. Cross-Cultural Differences in Empathy and Relevant Factors. Journal of Education Humanities and Social Sciences. 2023 Apr 5;10:197–202.

7. Editorial Team. Experiences Make People Happier Than Material Goods, Says University Of Colorado Prof [Internet]. 2004 [cited 2024 Apr 25]. Available from: https://www.sciencedaily.com/releases/2004/12/041219182811.htm

8. Ritter SM, Damian RI, Simonton DK, van Baaren RB, Dijksterhuis A. Diversifying Experiences Enhance Cognitive Flexibility. Journal of Experimental Social Psychology. 2012 Jul 1;48(4):961–4.

9. Dolcos F, Hohl K, Hu Y, Dolcos S. Religiosity and Resilience: Cognitive Reappraisal and Coping Self-Efficacy Mediate the Link between Religious Coping and Well-Being. Journal of Religion and Health. 2021 Aug;60(4):2892–905.

10. Prendergast S, Macphee D. Parental contributors to children's persistence and school readiness. Early Childhood Research Quarterly [Internet]. 2018 Jun 14 [cited 2024 Apr 25];45. Available from: https://www.researchgate.net/publication/325755060_Parental_contributors_to_children's_persistence_and_school_readiness

Dr. Robert Walker

A CHILD INTO THE WORLD

www.ingramcontent.com/pod-product-compliance
Lightning Source LLC
LaVergne TN
LVHW021958060526
838201LV00048B/1618